LIBRARY OF THE EARLY CIVILIZATIONS
EDITED BY PROFESSOR STUART PIGGOTT

Ancient Greek Literature

GREEK

IN

McGraw-Hill   Book

ANCIENT

LITERATURE

ITS LIVING CONTEXT

H. C. Baldry

Company · New York

DESIGNED AND PRODUCED BY THAMES AND HUDSON

CONTENTS

GENERAL EDITOR'S PREFACE

For a prehistorian to write a preface to a book on Greek literature may well be thought presumptuous, and indeed impious. Potsherds and not poems, house-plans and not Homer, are his business, and as a student of ancient material culture he would do well to stick to his last and cobble as best he may the recalcitrant leather scraps of excavation evidence. But is this taking a wholly fair view of either the archaeologist or of literature? The prehistorian, it is true, is dealing with accidentally preserved fragments of material artifacts produced by individuals and societies which, however skilled, did not include writing among their technologies. If they did, they would be the subject-matter of the historian, even if he did use archaeological as well as written evidence. But the prehistorian is (or should be) acutely conscious that much human activity is unrepresented, directly or indirectly, by archaeological evidence and, as Sir Mortimer Wheeler put it, 'the archaeologist may find the tub, but altogether miss Diogenes'. And the spoken word, language and literature, especially if the tradition is oral and unwritten, will be the cultural elements least likely to be represented by any form of material remains. Even if the vehicle of transmission is the written word, it may be difficult or impossible to correlate literature and archaeology.

But literature, just as much as tangible works of art, pots and pans, tools and weapons, is a social artifact. It comes into being, in whatever form it may take, because it is needed by the contemporary society, fulfilling the psychological requirements of individuals and of the group. No one composed an epic, a lyric or a drama without a receptive audience in mind. The composer or writer is himself a child of his age, and however individual his utterance it will reflect the cultural conditioning to which he has been subjected since birth. One of the great distinguishing characteristics of man as an animal is his capacity to create and transmit cultural traditions in parallel to those passed on by biological means—what Sir Peter Medawar has called non-genetic heredity. The expression of early Greek thought and feeling in the literature discussed in this book by Professor Baldry, changing in response to the changing needs of ancient Greek society, is the counterpart of the historical development from the end of the Mycenaean period to the rise of the Hellenistic Empire; vase painting from Geometric to Red-Figure styles, or sculpture from the Archaic *kouroi* to the altar of Pergamon.

Quite apart from the stylistic and emotive qualities of Greek literature, it is related to Greek life in another sense, telling of the social scene imperfectly known from material evidence. The *Iliad* and the *Odyssey*, for all their great poetic qualities, cannot have been unique in kind: they are the outstanding and only surviving examples of the epic poetry of High Bronze Age Europe, not so distant from the pre-Roman epics of the Celtic Iron Age that survived in the earliest Irish hero-tales, and appropriate to the world of an heroic aristocracy. Hesiod takes us into the smoky kitchen of an Iron Age farmstead which might as well be in Gaul as in Greece; Archilochus speaks for the randy soldier of fortune anywhere in the troubled times of ancient Europe. And without the poets and philosophers of Athens, the Parthenon, or a cup painted by Euphronios, would lose much of their significance.

The visual arts of the Greeks go hand in hand with their literature. Even if we are very uncertain in detail about the appearance of a Greek play during its original performance, our concept would be distressingly vague if we had no surviving theatres and no representational art in painting or sculpture. The fact that the Greeks drew on a long tradition of pictorial art concerned with the representation of people—as individuals, as symbols, or grouped in illustration of legend or anecdote—produced a visual commentary upon their literature. Greek art, in fact, like the sources in Western Asia, Egypt and Crete upon which it is based, is essentially literary in content, and not for nothing was it, in all these contexts, the products of literate peoples. Picture and pictogram were linked from the beginning. By contrast, the non-literate peoples of ancient Europe and Asia, whose oral compositions can only be inferred, developed abstract and non-representational art styles, like that of the Celts. The status of the earliest Greek vase paintings can be disputed—are they contemporary scenes, or do they illustrate legends? But here at least the legends are known, and how much more in doubt are we when occasionally in prehistoric Europe representational art (probably in fact Greek-inspired) appears, as on sixth-century BC pots from Hungary, where we see a lyre-player, dancers and a woman at her loom. A scene in a local village, or the tale of a rustic Penelope chanted by a Hallstatt *aoidos*? We shall never know, but in ancient Greece the arts spoke with one voice, and pictorial and literary evidence combine to present us with a vivid embodiment of one of the most remarkable intellectual episodes in the history of Western man.

STUART PIGGOTT

INTRODUCTION

In the past hundred years archaeology has added a new dimension to our picture of ancient Greece. Many of the remains of the civilization of antiquity had long been known; but since Schliemann's dramatic finds at Troy and Mycenae the continuing rediscovery of the early Greek world has enabled us to see and understand Greek life as never before. A people previously known mainly through its documents is now seen against the background of its material environment – its public buildings, its social amenities, its domestic details. Even the history of the Greek language has been extended far back into the second millennium BC by the brilliant decipherment of the Linear B script on tablets which the archaeologists brought to light: we now know that a form of Greek was spoken and written centuries before Homer, and study of the tablets along with inferences from archaeological remains is slowly revealing the character of the society from which they come.

What have these advances done for our understanding of Greek literature? Many papyrus finds have been made: tantalizing fragments of works hitherto unknown, sometimes a substantial passage, occasionally a complete work – a whole poem or even a play. All this, however, is a small addition to the aggregate we already possessed – the manuscripts dispersed among the museums, monasteries, and learned libraries of the world, treasured fruit of the labours of Byzantine and medieval copyists. In some ways growing knowledge of the material background from which it sprang has made us freshly aware how small this aggregate is. We see the surviving remnants of Greek literature, like the remains of Greek art and architecture and material civilization, as only a fraction of the wealth that once existed. Of scores of epic poems, we have a mere half dozen; of thousands of plays, forty-five; of countless speeches, enough to fill a few volumes. We know the names of many authors whose works have vanished completely, while from others, by quotation or on papyrus fragments, a few precious scraps have been preserved. It is some consolation that much of what we have now was regarded in ancient times as the best.

Our surviving documents are incomplete in another way on which archaeological discovery has thrown great emphasis. Our manuscripts record only the words of a literature which was once far more than the written word: they give us nothing of the minstrel's song, the action in the theatre, the excited political meeting. Yet we cannot fully understand the words themselves without some conception of the vivid occasions at which they were first delivered. Increasing awareness of the environment from which literature emerged has simultaneously made us more conscious of this deficiency and given us the means to overcome it. The surviving masterpieces of Greek poetry and prose need to be seen, and to some extent can be seen, as part of the living context which gave them birth. By combining the results of archaeology with statements in ancient commentators, implications drawn from the documents themselves, even parallels with other peoples, something can be done to recapture the whole occasion of which the words we now possess were once a part. In our time this is the way in which classical literature, so often criticized as dead, can be kept vividly alive; and to attempt to present it from this point of view, to place it by means of illustration and description in its living context, is the purpose of this book.

H.C.B.

CHAPTER ONE

Epic and its Background

Iliad and Odyssey

The earliest documents in Greek that can be called literature are the *Iliad* and the *Odyssey*, ascribed in antiquity,
along with others, to Homer. The Greek language was
already old and far developed when they were produced:
a likely date for both is the eighth century BC. Let us
look at the poems themselves before we consider the way
they arose or their relation to the background from which
they came.

The *Iliad* or 'poem about Ilion (Troy)', has as its *Ills 1, 2*
central theme a single episode in the last year of the
Trojan War – Achilles' angry withdrawal from the
struggle and its disastrous sequel:

Of the wrath of the son of Peleus – of Achilles – Goddess,
    sing –
That ruinous wrath, that brought sorrows past numbering
Upon the host of Achaea, and to Hades cast away
The valiant souls of heroes, and flung their flesh for prey
To hounds, and all the fowls of air . . .

1, 2 The abduction of
Helen before the Trojan
War was the subject of
vase-paintings as well as
epic. These come from
the fifth and the eighth
centuries BC respectively

3, 4 This great mixing-bowl, known from the name of its finder in 1845 as the François Vase, is the work of the painter Kleitias early in the sixth century. Its height is 26 inches. It has twice been reconstructed, once from the fragments originally discovered and again in 1900 after being shattered by a maniac. The various themes from heroic legend which it represents include a vividly drawn chariot-race (*right*) at the funeral games of Patroclus, described by Homer in the *Iliad* Book XXIII

The greatest fighter among the Achaeans (as Homer calls the Greeks) withdraws himself and his forces from the war and sulks in his tent because a captive girl has been taken from him by the Achaean leader, Agamemnon. In the great battle that follows the Trojans press the Achaeans hard, until Achilles is persuaded by his comrade Patroclus to lend him his armour and let him enter the fight. The scales are turned and the Trojans driven back; but Patroclus is killed, and the story moves to a climax as new armour is made for Achilles and he plunges into the conflict, killing the Trojan leader Hector in single combat and hauling the corpse behind his chariot back to the Achaean camp, where for eleven days it is kept unburied and dragged round Patroclus' tomb. Yet the poem ends on a note different from this savagery: the old Trojan king Priam visits Achilles and is given his son's body for burial. All this, the central theme of the epic, covers only a few weeks of the ten-year siege of Troy; but the poem's name is justified, for in the course of its fifteen thousand lines, by digression and reminiscence and prophecy, we hear of the whole course and background of the war.

Ills 3, 4, 75

Ill. 5

Ill. 6

This is a tale of blood and slaughter, glory and sorrow. The *Odyssey* ('poem about Odysseus'), four thousand lines shorter, has a less majestic but more adventurous

5, 6,   The climax of the *Iliad* is the death of the Trojan leader Hector when he is chased by Achilles around the walls of the city and finally faces him in single combat. Achilles drags the body away to the Achaean camp; but when Priam, king of Troy, comes to his tent and begs to be allowed to ransom the body of his son, Achilles receives the old man with sympathy and grants his request. In the fine vase-painting of the incident, *below*, Achilles' shield hangs above his couch and the dead Hector lies outstretched beneath it

7, 8 One of Priam's allies in the Trojan War was Memnon, a mythical king of Ethiopia, whose story was told in the *Aethiopis*, an epic poem now lost. The vase detail, *right*, shows one of his negro squires. The fine painting *below* from a sixth-century amphora by Exekias represents a quiet moment during the siege – Achilles (on the left) and Ajax playing a game. Note the elegance of detail in the treatment of hair and cloaks

9 This vase of the fifth century BC depicts Penelope and her son Telemachus at home on Ithaca during the long absence of Odysseus. Behind them stands the tapestry which Penelope said she must complete before making her choice between the many suitors for her hand and throne. As the *Odyssey* tells, in order to draw out the time until Odysseus should return she undid at night all that she had woven during the day

and romantic theme, recounting Odysseus' return home to Ithaca after the siege is over. The poet uses for the first time the device, imitated by Virgil and many others since, of starting his story in the middle and leaving the beginning to be told at a later stage. The narrative opens on the island of Ithaca ten years after the fall of Troy: many suitors have been vainly wooing Odysseus' wife Penelope and devouring the wealth of his kingdom, till at last his young son Telemachus goes to the Peloponnese to seek news of his father. Only at this point does the story turn to Odysseus himself in the midst of his travels and brings him to the strange land of Phaeacia, where he meets the princess Nausicaa and describes at her father's court his adventures since the Trojan War ended – his escapes from the land of the Lotus Eaters, the Cyclops, the Sirens, Circe, Scylla and Charybdis; his seven-year stay on an island as lover and prisoner of the nymph Calypso. From Phaeacia he eventually reaches Ithaca,

Ill. 9

Ills 10, 11
Ills 12–14

Ill. 15

16

10, 11   The story of the blinding of Polyphemus by
Odysseus and his men and their escape from the giant
tied under the bellies of his flock, vividly narrated in the
ninth book of the *Odyssey*, was a favourite subject in early
Greek art. These examples are a fragment of a wine-bowl
from Argos and an archaic bronze now at Delphi

12–14   Three very different portrayals of scenes from the *Odyssey*. On the side of a drinking-bowl, *above*, the enchantress Circe stands holding her magic potion among Odysseus' men, some of whom it has already turned into beasts. *Opposite*, a water-jar of the fifth century B C gives a lively representation of Odysseus' escape from the Sirens, whose singing lured sailors to destruction. To pass them in safety and yet hear their song, he hit on a device typical of his character: he stopped up his men's ears with wax and told them to tie him to the mast with strict orders not to set him free until the danger was past. The archaic picture of disaster by shipwreck, *opposite below*, comes from the neck of a wine-jug of the geometric period; whether it is inspired by the *Odyssey* or by real life we cannot tell. A man (Odysseus?) sits astride the keel of a capsized boat, while his drowned companions lie in the sea around him

Ills 16, 17   meets Telemachus, slaughters the suitors – a climax as dramatic and bloody as anything in the *Iliad* – and is reunited with Penelope. Again the telling ranges widely – not only through all the folk-lore and fiction which make up the hero's adventures, but through other sequels to the war.

Both *Iliad* and *Odyssey* are focused, like most Greek literature, on people: not on people in the mass, the armies or populations involved in the war and its aftermath, but on the individual actions and the utterances (often lengthy) of individual men and women, many of whom emerge as clearly though simply defined characters as the story goes on. This is indeed 'heroic' poetry, naturally centred on a single hero and one particular chain of incidents. But its most remarkable feature for

18

the modern reader is one which has been omitted in summarizing the poems: the continual presence of other beings than men and women, whose activities are interwoven in the story and indeed play the most decisive part in determining the course of events. Zeus and his quarrelsome family of gods and goddesses, divine inhabitants of Mount Olympus in the *Iliad*, a little more remote in the *Odyssey*, are definite and particular and individual characters in the narrative no less than Hector or Achilles. They are superhuman in their immortality and their magical powers, they can be majestic and

Ill. 18

15–17 The fifth-century vase-painter constantly turned to Homer for subject-matter. *Opposite*, Odysseus' old nurse Eurykleia washes her returned master's feet. In doing so she recognizes him by an old scar, but he stops her from revealing his secret. The two sides of the vase *below* powerfully represent the terrible climax of the story: Odysseus throws off his disguise and, with the bow that only he can draw, slaughters the suitors

18 The superhuman power of Homer's gods in their hours of majesty is magnificently portrayed in this bronze statue recovered from the sea off Artemisium less than forty years ago. Some authorities believe that it represents Poseidon, ruler of the seas, but it may well be Zeus himself

awe-inspiring; yet often their arbitrary interventions are prompted by motives and emotions that seem all too human. Sometimes, especially in the *Iliad*, the antics of Olympus provide comic relief from the grim scene on the Trojan plain. If Homer's men are sometimes god-like, his gods could hardly be more modelled in the image of man.

All this is related in hexameter verse in which Matthew Arnold rightly found the qualities of plainness of thought, plainness of speech, and rapidity. It is true that digressions are frequent and sometimes, especially in the *Odyssey*, there is a leisurely piling of incident on incident and speech on speech. But Homer's way of describing a scene or an action is swift and direct. His sentences are straightforward, putting one thing simply after another without any complex intertwining of subordinate clauses. There is little metaphor in his lines to confuse or delay our understanding. Where imagery is used, it is formally set out in the simile:

As when in heaven the stars about the moon
Look beautiful, when all the winds are laid,
And every height comes out, and jutting peak
And valley, and the immeasurable heavens
Break open to their highest, and all the stars
Shine, and the shepherd gladdens in his heart:
So many a fire between the ships and stream
Of Xanthus blazed before the towers of Troy.

Dramatic or lofty moments in the poems call forth more than two hundred brief pictures of this kind, in which the story-teller often seems to go beyond his comparison and dwell lovingly on details for their own sake. In this as in other features the Homeric style became a model for poets of later centuries – Virgil, for example, and Milton:

19 In this earliest extant representation of Homer, on a fourth-century coin from the island of Ios, there is no sign of the blindness later ascribed to him

Thick as autumnal leaves that strow the brooks
In Vallombrosa . . .

Arnold found one other principal virtue in the *Iliad* and *Odyssey*: 'nobility'. Although the word is out of fashion now, the quality is unmistakably there, and there throughout. Translators through the ages have found all Homer's qualities difficult to reproduce, but this is where they most commonly fail. His narrative is uneven in dramatic power and our interest sometimes flags: it never becomes trivial or cheap.

Who was Homer?

From the poems themselves we turn to their origin and background. How did the *Iliad* and *Odyssey* come into being in anything like their present form? Who was 'Homer', if such a poet existed at all? These questions have been keenly debated for centuries, and it is clear now that there is no simple answer. The poems themselves tell us nothing of their composer, and Greek tradition gave conflicting accounts of his date, his birthplace, and incidents of his life. The problem has been both complicated and rendered more fascinating by archaeological discovery. When Schliemann dug down into the site of Troy he believed he was revealing a historical background that would fit the *Iliad*, and in the graves which he unearthed at Mycenae he thought he had found the treasures of Agamemnon; but the matter has not proved so simple. Further advances in the archaeological study of early Greece have repeatedly confirmed that there was a historical reality behind the Homeric epics, but contradictions between the poems and the archaeological evidence have continually shown the complexity of the relationship between them. The decipherment of the Linear B tablets, revealing a bureaucratic society very different from the way of life in the

Ills 19, 20

Ills 22-24
Ill. 21

Ill. 26

20 From a marble relief of the second century B C which portrays the deification of Homer. The poet is being crowned by the World and Time. The monument symbolizes the unique reverence with which Homer continued to be regarded throughout antiquity in every part of the Greek-speaking world

Iliad or the *Odyssey*, has increased the difficulty of the problem instead of solving it.

Let us take the question of the origin of the poems first. Modern scholarship is agreed on one basic point: that the problem of authorship must be regarded as secondary, and the poems must be primarily seen as products of an evolutionary process. We can approach it best by going backwards in time.

In all but minor details our text of both epics goes back to the scholars of Alexandria in the third and second centuries B C. Before their work on it many versions must have existed, but variation was kept in check by the requirements of public performance: at festivals in a number of places, and above all at the Panathenaea held every four years at Athens, the two poems were recited to vast audiences by 'rhapsodes', who with their long staffs were familiar figures throughout Greece. For the purpose of the Panathenaic performances a stable text may well have been established as early as the sixth century B C.

Ill. 25

The rhapsode, however, is certainly not the beginning of the story. Further back still stands a more shadowy but more important figure – the 'aoidos', the singer; and

25

21, 22 Golden funeral masks which seem to bring us close to the Homeric heroes were among the treasures found by the German archaeologist, Schliemann, when he excavated the circle of shaft-graves at the citadel of Mycenae nearly a hundred years ago. The photograph *below*, taken during the excavation, includes the figures of Schliemann himself (right centre) and his wife (right foreground)

23, 24   The citadel of Mycenae, dominant power in the Aegean for at least two centuries and fortress of Agamemnon in Homer's epic, looks over the plain of Argos from its strategic position in the hills. A wall of huge Cyclopean masonry protected it and, *below*, the graves in which its kings were buried

25   The rhapsode, professional reciter of Homeric epic at great public festivals such as the Panathenaea at Athens, is splendidly portrayed on this amphora of the early fifth century B C

26 An example from Knossos in Crete of the Linear B tablets which have recently been deciphered and shown to contain a syllabic script which is the earliest written Greek. From the tablets and archaeology it is possible to reconstruct an outline picture of Mycenaean society

it is on him and his craft, illuminated by comparison with story-tellers of today in Yugoslavia and elsewhere, that the interest of Homeric scholars has centred in recent years. Such a singer is the blind Demodocus, described in the *Odyssey* itself at the feast at the Phaeacian Court:

> The crier soon came, leading that man of song
> whom the Muse cherished; by her gift he knew
> the good of life, and evil –
> for she who lent him sweetness made him blind.
> Pontonoos fixed a studded chair for him
> hard by a pillar amid the banqueters,
> hanging the taut harp from a peg above him,
> and guided up his hands upon the strings . . .
> In time, when hunger and thirst were turned away,
> the Muse brought to the minstrel's mind a song   *Ill. 27*
> of heroes whose great fame rang under heaven.

There is general agreement that the aoidos with his lyre is the source of the kind of verse narration which reaches its highest achievement in the *Iliad* and the *Odyssey*. When the telling of stories by such singers began, we do not know. It may well go back to Mycenaean times, but there is no direct evidence for this and none is likely to come to light. The syllabic writing which we find on the Linear B tablets from Knossos, Mycenae, and Pylos is   *Ill. 26* used only for record purposes – lists of officials, soldiers, or workers, inventories of furniture or stores, statements of dues owed to the ruler or offerings made to the gods.

There is no reason to suppose that this. script was ever used for poetry: on the contrary, there are good grounds for believing that narrative song, at any rate in the early stages of its development, must have been orally composed, delivered, and handed on. Just because the singer's art was unaided by writing, it involved both improvising new material and remembering the old; and in these twin needs lies the explanation of the main features of Homeric narrative: the hexameter framework; the language, an amalgam of dialect elements and invented forms which was never used in ordinary speech, but must have been shaped by generations of singers to suit the metrical framework; the stereotyped word-groups or formulae constantly employed to fill this or that part of the hexameter line. Repetition, an essential aspect of the improviser's technique, leaves its mark everywhere in the two epics, whether a noun-plus-adjective formula ('stock epithet') is repeated, such as 'swift-footed Achilles', 'resourceful Odysseus', 'the wine-dark sea'; or a stock line recurs to describe a familiar event:

But when early Dawn appeared, the rosy-fingered . . .

Some whole sets of lines do service more than once – a message, for example, or an account of preparations for the fight.

The Date of Homer
With the help of these means a growing body of verse stories must have been created and handed down, until recital by rhapsodes replaced the singer's chant and (not necessarily at the same time) oral composition gave way to the use of writing, now in the alphabetic script which had come into being in the eighth century or earlier. Plainness of thought and speech and rapidity of movement would be their natural attributes. But at what stage

27 On this funeral oil-jar one of the Muses, goddesses of poetry and the other arts, sits playing her lyre on a rock which bears the name of Helicon, the Muses' sacred mountain

in this long evolution did the *Iliad* and *Odyssey* emerge in something like their present form?

There can be no certain answer to the question. Some scholars see the beginning of festival recitations as the occasion which called such monumental poems into being; others place their creation in the time of the aoidos, as much as two centuries before the coming of the rhapsode. Some maintain that works of such length cannot have been composed or handed on without the use of writing; according to others, oral composition is more credible, and a period of oral transmission may have followed. Few now suppose that epics of such magnitude, far surpassing the ordinary singer's tale in unity of theme and poetic quality, could be the product of a mere compiler of lays; but while some believe in a single 'Homer', study of the differences between the poems points rather to two poets of genius, separated perhaps by several

◁ 28 This picture from a South-Italian vase burlesques the ambushing of Dolon by Odysseus and Diomedes. The story is thought to be a late addition to the *Iliad*

29 A tablet with cuneiform script, dated about 1300 BC, from the Hittite capital Ḥattušaš in the middle of Asia Minor. The arrowed line refers to the 'greeting gifts of the king of Aḫḫijavā'. Such Hittite references confirm the existence and power of Homer's Achaeans

generations, the second of whom sought to emulate the achievement of the first. Both must have incorporated in their work much narrative material handed down from the past; and some episodes – the ambushing of Dolon, for example, in the *Iliad*, and Odysseus' visit to the world of the dead – were probably added at a later date.

Ill. 28

Amid these uncertainties one vital point is now established: both epics belong to a late stage in the evolution of such narrative verse, when the singer's art was no longer crude but polished to its highest perfection. The simile, at any rate in its elaborated form, is now thought to be an enrichment added in the final phase of the development of his technique. This lateness goes a long way towards explaining the relation of 'Homer' to history, as it has been revealed by research since Schliemann began his excavations at Troy, the mound of Hissarlik, nearly a century ago.

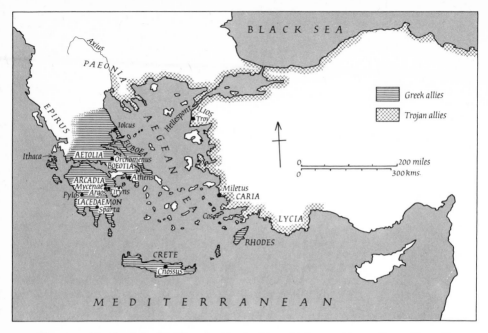

30 The second book of the *Iliad* lists the Greek cities which sent ships to Troy. Many Mycenaean cities are named, and the area corresponds well with the extent of Mycenaean settlement. A similar list of Trojan allies includes most of the coast towns of Asia Minor and northern Greece

Homer and History

Ill. 29

Ill. 23

Cuneiform texts discovered at the ancient Hittite capital in the middle of Asia Minor refer to a country called Aḫḫijavā, powerful enough to hold territorial rights in a coastal area to the west, which the Hittite king visits. The date is about 1300 BC. Aḫḫijavā, there can be little doubt, is the land of the Achaiwoi, Homer's Achaeans, and the Hittite texts are external confirmation of their existence and their power. Clearly the thirteenth century is the time to which the *Iliad* looks back. Hundreds of years before this the Greeks had come down from the north, and eventually they had overcome the power of Minoan Crete. Now the centre of power lay at Mycenae, the richest, most magnificent, and most strongly fortified city in Greece, whose king is likely to have been overlord of the surrounding area and even of other parts of the

34

31, 32 The boars' tusk helmet described in the *Iliad* is illustrated by an ivory plaque with a Mycenaean warrior found on Delos and an actual helmet from a Knossos tomb

Aegean. This is the situation reflected in Homer, especially in the second book of the *Iliad*, which lists the places in Greece that sent ships to Troy. The catalogue corresponds remarkably closely to the pattern of settlement which archaeology has revealed. The riches of Mycenae, regarded as a fairy-tale until the archaeologist's spade brought them to light, are part of Homer's picture, and so are many material details which recent discovery has confirmed – the helmet covered with pieces of boar's tusk, for example, which is described with great precision in the *Iliad*. If the two great epics were composed late in the development of narrative poetry several centuries after Mycenae's period of power, when the whole face of Greece had been transformed by invasions and migrations and political change, it is not surprising that other

Ill. 30
Ill. 21

Ills 31, 32

35

aspects of their picture do not correspond with what archaeology reveals, or that their portrayal of Achaean life, with its concentration on the heroic individual, has little in common with the bureaucratic society of the Linear B tablets. Because the poems combine traditional material of various periods, they reflect not one stage of social development but several; and where tradition failed, the poet's imagination must have filled the gap.

What of the Trojan War itself? Of the various settlements on the site near the Dardanelles which Schliemann began to excavate in 1870, the one known to archaeologists as VII A seems to have been destroyed by an enemy within the period in which Greek tradition placed the siege of Troy. That the struggle took place there can be little doubt. Its size and character and the identity of the participants are questions which perhaps will never be settled – whether it was indeed a military adventure under Mycenaean leadership aimed at seizing the Dardanelles as a step towards further conquest; or whether invaders from the north whom the Egyptians called 'the sea peoples' overran Troy on their way southwards and captured it with the help of Greeks whom legend later

Ill. 33

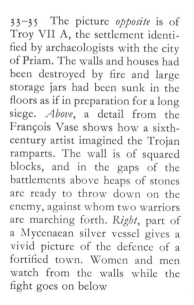

33–35 The picture *opposite* is of Troy VII A, the settlement identified by archaeologists with the city of Priam. The walls and houses had been destroyed by fire and large storage jars had been sunk in the floors as if in preparation for a long siege. *Above*, a detail from the François Vase shows how a sixth-century artist imagined the Trojan ramparts. The wall is of squared blocks, and in the gaps of the battlements above heaps of stones are ready to throw down on the enemy, against whom two warriors are marching forth. *Right*, part of a Mycenaean silver vessel gives a vivid picture of the defence of a fortified town. Women and men watch from the walls while the fight goes on below

36 This remarkable picture of the Trojan Horse is from the neck of a seventh-century amphora from the island of Mykonos. With typical archaic disregard of realism the artist shows the Greeks within the horse who are invisible to the Trojans outside

Ills 34-36

transformed into leaders of the attack. Whatever the truth, it is clear that by the time of the composition of the *Iliad* this episode in the remote past of the Greeks has been enlarged and glorified far beyond historical reality. Events which must have belonged to different times and places have all become incidents of this one great campaign. The siege has been lengthened to ten years. The armies involved have swollen to an impossible size: although the remains of Troy cover only a few acres, the *Iliad* numbers the defenders at fifty thousand men. The leaders on both sides have become supermen with a physique far surpassing the strength of the poet's contemporaries. Ajax's shield of seven oxhides and a layer of metal must have weighed over twenty stone.

37 Hector bids farewell to his wife Andromache before his fatal combat with Achilles. This version on a wine-bowl of the sixth century B C leaves out the nurse and child who complete the scene as Homer describes it in the sixth book of the *Iliad*

The historical background to the *Odyssey* is more obscure. But its hero's travels and the wanderings of other Achaean leaders which it relates may well be seen as a legendary and poetical memory, supplemented by folklore and fantasy, of the migrations which new invaders generally known as the 'Dorians' forced upon the Greeks not many decades after the Trojan War. Among them was a great movement from Attica and elsewhere on the mainland across the Aegean to its eastern shore; and according to tradition it was among the settlers there known as 'Ionians' that 'Homer' eventually arose to recount the stories of their glorious past.

I have tried to show that the distance in time of the *Iliad* and the *Odyssey* from the Trojan War and the migrations helps to explain their relationship to history. If the two epics are seen as the climax of a long evolution, other features of them are also more easily understood: their treatment, for example, of the gods. In the course of centuries the Olympian deities have been adapted to the storyteller's needs. They have been humanized and individualized until they can play their part in the narrative alongside the mortal characters; along with the hexameter and the repeated phrase, they have become part of the singer's technique.

Equally linked with the poems' remoteness from the events of which they tell is their attitude to man. Although they are concerned with a war and its sequel, they do not take sides: Achaeans and Trojans alike are seen as subject to the common lot of mortality – a fate which the hero must undergo no less than the commoner, for all his prowess and pride. There is no mawkish sentiment in Homeric epic: its scenes of suffering and death are often too starkly realistic for the modern palate. But it does share with other great poetry the quality of compassion for the human lot. The note is struck in such scenes as the farewell of Hector to his wife and infant son, or in brief moments like the glimpse of happier days as Achilles later pursues Hector round the walls of Troy:

Ills 5, 6

38 In this drawing from an archaic vase now lost, Achilles lies dead while a struggle takes place over his corpse. The story of his death was not told in the *Iliad*, but in later epic

There by the springs are roomy washing-troughs,
Fine troughs of stone, where in old days of peace
Or ever the sons of the Achaeans came,
The ladies and fair daughters of the Trojans
Would wash their shining robes. Thereby they ran,
One fleeing, one pursuing.

39 Two details from a Caeretan water-jar with the infant Hermes feigning sleep, having stolen and hidden the cows of Apollo, whilst an argument ensues as to who was the thief

Pity for human frailty is most strongly present in the *Iliad*, and finds its greatest expression in the tragic figure of Achilles, the mighty warrior foredoomed to an early death, whose individual drama of moral degradation and redemption is seen against the background of the larger tragedy of Troy itself.

Ill. 38

Homer's Legacy

The influence of these first masterpieces is evident in nearly all later Greek poetry. For epic they were accepted as models which all must imitate but none could equal: narrative hexameters continued to be composed in Greek until Byzantine times, but it was left to Roman Virgil, still following the same tradition, to produce a work worthy of comparison with Homer.

The *Odyssey* seems to have been soon followed by a large number of shorter poems using the same metre and technique, which centuries later were arranged into an 'Epic Cycle' covering the whole range of myth and legend. From all this only a few pages of fragments survive today. Time has been kinder to thirty-four examples of the 'Homeric Hymn' – a form which began as a brief tribute to a deity before epic recitation, but itself developed into an epic narrative relating with great charm, if not with full Homeric power, the story of Demeter and Persephone or Apollo or Hermes or Aphrodite.

Ill. 61

Ill. 39

CHAPTER TWO

Poetry of Changing Times

The Individual Speaks

Most of these poems were associated, at any rate for a time, with the name of Homer. Others, including the still extant *Theogony*, were ascribed to Hesiod, commonly regarded by the Greeks as Homer's contemporary. But Hesiod's best-known poem, the strange eight-hundred-line medley known as the *Works and Days*, has a tone and purpose very different from epic narrative. The hexameter line, the epic language and formulae are still there, and so also is legend – the story of Pandora, and of man's degeneration from the Golden Age. The poet's object, however, is not to entertain an audience, but to advise and instruct the countryman on ways of work and lucky and unlucky days. Above all, the *Works and Days* is a *personal* poem: the author emerges clearly as a disgruntled farmer of the mainland territory of Boeotia, who rails at his brother, Perses, over the unfairness of a judgment dividing their father's farm:

Ill. 40

Perses, set these thoughts firmly in your heart.
Strife that delights in mischief must not keep
Your heart from work, as with listening ear you watch
The court-house wrangles.

40   This sowing and ploughing scene on a vase of the sixth-century B C probably has a religious significance, but it illustrates well the hard farming life which was the background to Hesiod's poem, the *Works and Days*

Homer's impersonal narrative has been replaced by personal feeling, the heroic past by the harsh realities of the present. The heroes we meet in the *Iliad* and the *Odyssey* are full of zest for life and action – perhaps all the more so because they are constantly aware that violent death may cut life short. In Hesiod we find a different spirit. The Heroic Age, he tells us, no less than the Ages of Gold and Silver and Bronze, is past: this is the Age of Iron, in which life is grim and hard. The *Works and Days* reflects the atmosphere of a small community filled with petty strife and engaged in a continual struggle to wrest a living from the land. We are not far away from the wave of colonization which sent Greeks overseas from many communities in search of more and better land, nor from revolutionary conflict and political change. But neither of these solutions is mentioned by Hesiod. His emphasis falls on the need for the farmer to fill his barns by labour and thrift, and on grumbling discontent with the 'crooked judgments' of the local 'kings'. The idea of justice, already more strongly present in the *Odyssey* than in the *Iliad*, becomes a repeated theme in Hesiod, and for him Zeus is never a figure of fun, but the guardian of the right. Unlike Homer, Hesiod is a poet with individual feelings to express and a conscious message to proclaim.

This aspect of the *Works and Days* is a foretaste of all the personal poetry that arose out of the conflicts and discontents of the seventh and sixth centuries B C – topical expressions of individual reaction to the events

43

of the day which often strike a strangely modern note. Where Hesiod retained the hexameter, others turned to forms better suited to the utterance of emotion or thought: iambics, for example, nearer in rhythm and diction to ordinary speech and later to be used as the normal dialogue metre in drama; or the elegiac couplet, created by adding a shorter line to the hexameter, which subsequently became the accepted medium for epigrams and especially for epitaphs, and so gave the word 'elegy' to European literature. Although verse of this type must have been transmitted in writing, little now survives – only brief and tantalizing glimpses, in various parts of the Greek world, of the mental and political ferment of the time. It will be worth while to glance at a few examples of the scanty fragments we possess, in which we can see a little of the conflicts between cities, the struggle of settlers against non-Greek 'barbarians', the strife within the community of nobles against 'tyrants' or 'the good' against 'the base'.

From the island of Paros came the wanderer-poet Archilochus, son of a noble father but a slave mother, roused to bitter invective when prevented from marrying *Ill. 41* a well-born girl, driven to a mercenary soldier's life but with no illusions about the glory of war:

> A perfect shield bedecks some Thracian now;
>   I had no choice: I left it in a wood.
> Ah, well, I saved my skin, so let it go!
>   A new one's just as good.

He has a rough camp cynicism which scoffs at foppish generals:

> I hate the lanky officer, stiff-standing, legs apart,
>   Whose cut of hair and whisker is his principal renown;
> I prefer the little fellow with his bigness in his heart,
>   And let his legs be bandy, if they never let him down.

41 Archilochus was a mercenary soldier in the seventh century BC. On this Attic amphora, dated a century or more later, Greek infantrymen with their great helmets and round shields and spears advance alongside tall-capped Scythian mercenaries armed with bows and quivers of arrows. Mercenaries appear little in Greek literature, but played an ever-increasing part in Greek warfare

Archilochus mentions an eclipse of the sun which took place in 648 BC – our first exact date in the history of Greek literature. We are not very far in time from Homer or Hesiod, but in feeling he often seems remote from either Achilles or the Boeotian farm. Our small remains of his large and varied output confirm the comment of a Roman critic: 'the greatest force of expression, a phrasing not only telling but terse and vigorous, and abundance of blood and muscle'. The loss of most of his work leaves one of the worst gaps in the literature of the ancient world.

Perhaps half a century later at Colophon, on the eastern side of the Aegean, Mimnermus strikes another note. In the best known fragment of his poetry the theme is 'Gather ye roses while ye may'. Better an early death than the dreary prospect of old age:

We are as leaves in jewelled springtime growing
  That open to the sunlight's quickening rays;
So joy we in our span of youth, unknowing
  If God shall bring us good or evil days.
Two fates beside thee stand; the one hath sorrow,
  Dull age's fruit, that other gives the boon
Of Death, for youth's fair flower hath no tomorrow,
  And lives but as a sunlit afternoon.

At Athens early in the sixth century a very different figure, the statesman Solon, uses verse to declare his views and policies where a modern politician might write pamphlets in prose. He warns the citizens, for example, of the need for vigilance against dictatorship:

As on the fiery lightning followeth the thunder,
  As from the cloudrack comes the driving hail and snow,
From men of power comes a city's ruin; so it falls under
  A despot – by their folly its folk to bondage go.
Once a man is exalted, hard he grows to restrain.
Already the time is on ye to see that issue plain.

Two glimpses of poets of the late sixth century will serve to illustrate the variety of individual thought and feeling which our few remains of this early verse reflect. One is the conservative landowner Theognis, of Megara, not far from Athens. He complains in bitter elegiacs that cross-breeding between rich and poor is ruining the community and the lower orders no longer know their place; and later, dispossessed and exiled, he remembers the home he has lost:

I heard the crane cry unto men his greeting,
  To tell them it was time to drive the plough;
Ah, friend! he set my sorry heart a-beating,
  For others have my fertile acres now.

Just the opposite of Theognis is the radical thinker Xenophanes, wandering critic of the accepted traditions

42 Unlike Homeric epic, the poetry described in this chapter is likely to have been written down from the first. The earliest examples of Greek alphabetic script are found on fragments of Geometric pottery. This jug, from the end of the eighth century BC, was (probably with its contents) a prize in a dancing contest. The inscription reads 'He whose performance is best among all the dancers shall have me'

and conventions of the day. He attacked the glorification of victors in the games which was to be one of the main subjects of Pindar's poetry. Most of all he condemned the epic picture of the gods:

> Stealing, adultery, and base deceit,
>   All that among men brings rebuke and blame,
> Homer and Hesiod to the gods ascribe.

Other fragments of Xenophanes anticipate much later ideas by ridiculing the conception of gods in the image of men:

> The Aethiop's gods are black, snub-nosed;
> Blue-eyed, red-haired the Thracian's.

Or again:

> Could horses, oxen, lions hold
>   The tools to paint and carve like men,
> They'd make the gods in their own mould
>   Gods would be horses and oxen then.

47

Dance and Lyric Song

Elegiacs and iambics, like the hexameter, lost their musical accompaniment and became poetry to be spoken or read. But there were other verse forms which always retained the character of song; for them, melody was essential, whether accompanied by the lyre (hence 'lyric' poetry) or more rarely by the flute. Some were for solo performance, and involved only words and music; in other types a third element was included – the dance. Vase paintings with their many pictures of dancing groups show what a vital part the dance played in Greek religion and Greek life. To modern minds trained on bookish notions of literature dancing may seem to have little to do with poetry, but to the Greeks the connection between the two was obvious and of great importance. The combination of dance and song must have gone back to the earliest times. In Homer's world it is already long established, and different occasions call it forth in different forms. At a grape harvest, for example, while boys and girls carry the grapes in baskets,

Ill. 42

Ills 45, 46

> in their midst a boy
> Made lovely music with his ringing lyre,
> And sang to it the pretty Linos song
> In his clear treble, while the rest kept time
> With shouts and song, and followed up behind
> On dancing feet.

Ills 43, 44

Here the lyre-player sings, the others dance. Elsewhere, usually as part of some ritual act, it is the whole dancing chorus that performs the song.

The tradition reflected in these Homeric scenes bore rich fruit in the seventh and sixth centuries BC, although its appeal to later antiquity was slight and little has survived. Here perhaps more than anywhere else in Greek literature we are handicapped in our appreciation of what survives by ignorance of the performance as a whole of

43, 44 Dancing chorus of young men and girls, from the neck of an Attic amphora from the eighth or seventh century BC. The dance, so often pictured on vases, played a great part in the development of Greek poetry

which the words were part. We know scarcely anything about the music of the songs, and still less about the dance. Even the text exists for the most part only in damaged and problematic remnants, but there is enough to reveal at any rate the verbal magic of some of this early poetry.

Our earliest example, already far removed from traditional folk-song, comes in the late seventh century BC from Sparta, almost the only literary evidence of the civilization that flourished there before military austerity took its place. Recovered on papyrus in Egypt in 1855, it is part of one of the choral songs for girls for which the poet Alcman was well known – a hymn sung by ten girls to a goddess before dawn. In spite of many difficulties of interpretation, we can still appreciate the music of Alcman's words, the liveliness, the charming quaintness of comparisons such as the chorus use of their leader,

whose beauty seems as high and rare
as if with brutes one should compare
a sturdy thundering horse, a champion,
of winged dreams the son.

45, 46 Two very different vase-paintings illustrate the prominent place of the dance in Greek religious and social life. *Left*, a vase from the Spartan settlement of Tarentum in southern Italy shows boy and girl dancers taking part in the late summer festival known as the Carneia. The vase dates from about 410 BC. *Opposite*, is a simple scene from a Boeotian jug roughly contemporary: two boys dance under a trellis of leaves to the music of a double pipe

Ill. 47

From the prosperous island of Lesbos, another centre of intellectual and cultural life until it came under the domination of Persia, we possess bits and pieces of the work of two remarkable poets of the early sixth century BC. Alcaeus and Sappho composed many types of verse, but their distinctive contribution to ancient literature, perhaps developed from popular beginnings, was the simple short-stanza song for an individual singer. Alcaeus is a bitter aristocratic opponent of the 'tyrant' Pittacus. Posterity came to regard Pittacus as one of the Seven Wise Men, but to Alcaeus he is a political anathema:

This upstart Pittacus, this base-born fool . . .

Ill. 48

Alcaeus' verse is topical, vigorous, masculine, whether he utters a stream of invective against the 'tyrant' or a call to drown such cares in wine:

> To woe the heart must not give in,
> In grief's no help. One medicine,
> My friend, alone is fit –
> Wine – and get drunk on it.

47 Alcaeus and Sappho, the two famous poets of the island of Lesbos, are pictured together on this vase. A poetess was a ready subject for scandal or romance, and stories of both kinds gathered round her name later; but there is no hint of them in this portrait, which belongs to the early fifth century B C

48   Wine is a favourite topic with Alcaeus and other early Greek poets, and the background to many of their songs is the drinking party, though not perhaps carried to such excess as the one portrayed above – a picture from a sixth-century wine jug

Sappho, born a few years later than Alcaeus, was the one outstanding poetess of Greece. The fact that she wrote love-songs, including some to members of her own sex, has had strange results for both ancient and modern conceptions of her and her background; and it is doubtful whether scandal (which turned her into a prostitute) or romance (which made her leap to her death, heartbroken, from a cliff) or ideas and prejudices about 'Lesbianism' have done more to obscure the historical reality. The few facts we have about her are simple. Like Alcaeus she belonged to the aristocracy, and went into exile with them as a young girl. After returning to Lesbos she married and had a daughter. She set up a school (apparently one of several on the island) where the daughters of the well-to-do could learn such higher arts as music and song. Her 'school' centred on a religious cult, but it was no nunnery. Its deity was Aphrodite, goddess of beauty and love; and the girls learned not to ignore physical loveliness but to seek it, not to renounce marriage but to prepare for it in heart and mind. Isolated by custom from men until the time of marriage, they inevitably turned their emotions towards each other; above all, towards Sappho herself.

For Sappho it is not power or political strife that matters but the individual: her own inward emotions,

the beauty of someone she loves – her own daughter, perhaps, worth more to her than all the riches of the neighbouring kingdom of Lydia:

> I have a child; so fair
> As golden flowers is she,
> My Cleïs, all my care.
> I'd not give her away
> For Lydia's wide sway
> Nor lands men long to see.

Our fragments of Sappho's work – we possess only one poem, a prayer to Aphrodite, complete – have a seemingly effortless craftsmanship, a radiant simplicity, a delicacy of imagery which vanish all too easily in translation. Rossetti's version of a simile describing a young bride captures something of these qualities, yet seems laboured in comparison with the original:

Like the sweet apple which reddens upon the topmost
  bough,
A-top on the topmost twig – which the pluckers forgot
  somehow –
Forgot it not, nay, but got it not, for none could get it
  till now.

Ill. 49

The simplicity of these Lesbian poets, but neither Alcaeus' vigour nor Sappho's depth, reappears two generations later in the songs of Anacreon, court poet of several of the 'tyrants' of the day. A typical stanza illustrates his charming fantasy:

Ills 50, 51

> Once more the Lad with golden hair
> His purple ball across the air
>   Flings at me, true to aim;
> And light her broidered slippers go,
> That Lesbian lass – my playfellow
>   As Love would set the game.

50, 51   Attic vase-paintings depicting Anacreon, poet of wine and love, with two boon-companions. His name on the version *above*, from a much-damaged oil-jar, makes the identification certain. In the version *below* his companions are represented wearing women's dress and hats, and one carries a parasol. Anacreon visited Athens late in the sixth century B C, and this wine-jar, produced about that time, may be a satire on the effeminacy of the poet and his associates

The Choral Ode

In contrast with such slight and ephemeral verse stands the splendour and complexity of choral song as we find it in the early fifth century in the odes of Pindar. There were material causes for this culminating achievement. The patronage of wealthy aristocrats and 'tyrants' resulted in the emergence of professional songwriters who could pay to men the eulogies previously bestowed on the gods; and they made use of every means – the development of musical technique, for example, and the adaptation of epic legend – to further the elaboration of their art. In such a context originality, rather than tradition, was at a premium, and in spite of the division of choral song into fixed types its composers differed greatly in their handling of it. In the early sixth century, a little later than Alcman, Stesichorus seems to have used it mainly as a vehicle for narrative, reshaping within this different poetic framework much of the rich heritage of legend which 'Homer' and 'Hesiod' had made known throughout Greece. Other choral poets sometimes followed his example; more often they assumed knowledge of the familiar stories in their hearers and filled their odes with allusions to them which make the surviving remains difficult for the modern reader. But here, as elsewhere in Greek literature, there is no acceptance of a dogmatic tradition. The poet was free to decorate the myths with picturesque detail of his own invention, to remove crudities, to introduce new twists and turns in which the writers of tragedy later sometimes saw better dramatic material than in the epic versions. Surprisingly, choral song was also the vehicle of the composer's own thoughts and feelings, so that for all its ritual and traditional background the poet's individual personality stands out. Although only fragments survive from the work of Simonides at the beginning of the fifth century, we can sharply distinguish his rationalism from the mysticism of

Pindar: he brought to choral poetry the same smoothness
of style and skill in the choice of words which he showed
in his epigrams – the famous epitaph, for example, on the
Spartans who fell at Thermopylae:

> Go tell the Spartans, thou who passest by,
> That here obedient to their laws we lie.

Simonides' nephew Bacchylides, the last choral poet of
distinction, is consistently graceful and polished, though
he rarely rises to a higher level. But most of the odes we
now possess are the work of the Boeotian aristocrat
Pindar, and these shape our idea of the genre.

Pindar wrote many kinds of choral song; what we now
have complete is his *Epinician* or *Victory Odes*, composed
for ceremonies in honour of victors at the Games. The
great stadia still to be seen at Delphi and elsewhere bear
witness to the importance of the great athletic festivals
in Greek life. Four main festivals were held: at Olympia
and Nemea in the Peloponnese, at Delphi, and at Corinth.
Athletes came from all over the Greek world to compete;
and if they returned victorious, their homecoming was
splendidly celebrated. All this is understandable enough

Ill. 53

Ill. 52

Ills 54, 55

52, 53   The background to Pindar's *Victory Odes* was the great athletic festivals, the origin of our Olympic Games. The contests provided many subjects for vase-paintings (*opposite above*). The great stadium beneath the cliffs at Delphi, in which the Pythian Games were held, is still used today. The seats of the judges can be seen in the middle of the third row

to a century familiar with the modern Olympic Games and the World Cup. What seems strange, and is typical of the difference in the place of poetry in our world and in ancient Greece, is that the victor's return was celebrated with choral song. The odes which Pindar composed for such occasions are divided into four groups – *Olympian*, *Pythian*, *Nemean*, and *Isthmian* – corresponding to the four festivals. Praise of the victor and his family and city is only one of the threads which Pindar skilfully weaves together: with the particular occasion he combines generalization and legend, and at the same time uses the chorus as mouthpiece of his personal feelings and beliefs. Each ode has its own complex metrical pattern; and through all runs a magnificence of language and splendour of imagery which may be illustrated by the sublime description of the power of music, inspiration of the dance, at the beginning of the first *Pythian*:

O lyre of gold, Apollo's
Treasure, shared with the violet-wreathed Muses,
The light foot hears you, and the brightness begins:
Your notes compel the singer
When to lead out the dance
The prelude is sounded on your trembling strings.
You quench the warrior Thunderbolt's everlasting flame:
On God's sceptre the Eagle sleeps,
Drooping his swift wings on either side,
The King of Birds.
You have poured a cloud on his beak and head,
    and darkened his face:
His eyelids are shut with a sweet seal.
He sleeps, his lithe back heaves:
Your quivering song has conquered him.

Pindar's poetry is difficult for the modern reader to appreciate and raises baffling problems for the translator, yet it is one of the greatest glories of Greek literature.

54, 55 Chariot races were a prominent feature of the Games, and they often provide material for the artist as well as the poet. The Syracusan coin on the right, from the last decade of the fifth century BC, shows a galloping four-horse chariot. Beneath the horses' forelegs is a fallen turning-post, while above them a winged victory approaches to crown the driver. *Below*, the speed and excitement of the race are brilliantly captured on a vase lid dated about 500 BC

CHAPTER THREE

Athens and the Theatre

The City

Up to this point the Greek literature known to us comes from many different places. In the fifth and fourth centuries B C, from which far more survives, it has one main source, the city of Athens; and here we can study an aspect of it which is only dimly apparent elsewhere – its relation to the society in which it was produced. In the modern world the creation and enjoyment of literature are the marginal occupation of a minority, and make little impact on the outlook or activities of the people as a whole. The secret of Athens' amazing literary achievement was its central place not only in education but in the life of the adult community, which took it for granted that literature deeply affects society and is something with which society must be concerned. Plato's proposal to expel poets from his Utopia springs from the assumption that poetry is a force which can preserve or wreck the welfare of the state.

Athens was the largest of the Greek city-states in the fifth century B C. At the height of her power and splendour she probably had a total population of about 300,000, of whom some 40,000 were citizens (adult males of Athenian parentage who with their families formed nearly half of the community), perhaps 110,000 were slaves, and the rest were Greeks resident in the city with their families, though not of Athenian descent. Why did this city, of no great size or wealth by twentieth-century standards, give to the world within a few decades not only some of its finest art and architecture – the sculptures of Phidias, the magnificence of the Parthenon – but also literature which has never been surpassed?

Ills 57, 58

The answer certainly does not lie in the importance of books at Athens. There is some evidence of the spread of books and reading there towards the close of the fifth century, and we shall see that some works – Thucydides' *History*, for example – are likely to have been written for readers rather than an audience. Nevertheless, literature remained predominantly oral. Behind the genres that now flourished lay the part played by the spoken word in a community which enjoyed leisure as a result of slavery, used the easiest of all meeting-places, the open air, and took an uninhibited delight in the gift of speech. A walk round the remains of the ancient city and brief study of her monuments makes it easy to understand how such a community could give birth to so many masterpieces of the spoken word, only a fraction of which, be it remembered, we now possess. From the democratic assembly on the Pnyx and the law-courts came the eloquence of the orators; from talk in the market-place (now recently excavated) and the streets and the sports-grounds, the philosophic dialogue. Most important and significant of all was the role of poetry in the great religious festivals, climaxes in the city's life. At the festival of Athena in the summer, preceded by the ritual procession immortalized in the sculptures of the Parthenon frieze, rhapsodes recited the epics of Homer. In a dialogue of Plato one of them gives us a brief glimpse of the exciting impact of his performance on the audience:

Ill. 56

Ill. 57

Whenever I look down at them from the platform I

56 The great rock of the Acropolis still dominates the city of Athens. The above view of it is from the Pnyx. The procession in honour of Athena moved up to her temple, the Parthenon, along the Sacred Way from the recently excavated Agora. The entrance to the Acropolis, known as the Propylaea, can be seen on the left, and the Parthenon further to the right

see them weeping, gazing wildly at me, marvelling at what they hear.

Elsewhere, at festivals in honour of Dionysus or Bacchus, god of fertility and especially of wine, performers of choral song competed for the judges' approval under the patronage of the whole citizen audience; and alongside these contests had grown up competition in another genre which was itself an offshoot of choral song – drama, the greatest of Athens' contributions to the rise of European literature.

The Festivals of Dionysus

Ills 59, 60 Two main annual festivals of Dionysus provided the setting for drama. At the Great Dionysia, the spring festival of the god, and again on a minor scale at his

57, 58 Two pictures of the Parthenon as the chequered course of history has left it. The great temple was built in the fifth century B C by Ictinus and Callicrates, and Phidias was the sculptor of the forty-foot gold and ivory statue of Athena which it housed. In the picture *below* can be seen part of the frieze depicting the Panathenaic procession

59, 60 The worship of Dionysus or Bacchus, god of wine and of drama, was a favourite subject in art as well as literature. In the vase-painting, *left*, women worshippers of the god pour and ladle wine at a table in front of his image. *Below*, a husband comes home late from the Anthesteria, the god's festival in March when the wine-jars from last autumn's grapes were opened and there was drinking throughout the city. He beats on the door while his wife hurries nervously with a lamp to let him in

61   This delightful and beautifully composed painting by Exekias, dated about 540 B C, probably illustrates a story of Dionysus told in one of the Homeric Hymns. Captured by pirates, the god revealed himself and caused a vine to grow up round the mast. The terrified pirates jumped overboard and were turned into dolphins. The ship's prow represents a boar's head

winter festival, the Lenaea, several days were devoted to contests in tragedy and comedy. The judges were ten citizens picked to give a verdict on behalf of all: they were selected by an elaborate procedure to avoid bribery, but no doubt they were influenced by the reactions which the mass audience was not slow to show. The performances were state subsidized in two ways: partly because the state provided its citizens with the money to buy their theatre tickets, specimens of which still exist; and also because the production was financed in the same way as warships, by wealthy citizens who were obliged to give this service to the community unless they could prove that others were wealthier still. It is significant that drama ranked alongside armaments for subsidy through this simple form of income tax.

In the modern world drama is generally a secular affair, which has often come under the disapproval of the church. The Great Dionysia was a spectacular ritual occasion, at which the chief seat of honour was given to Dionysus' priest; a state holiday so general that even

62–65 The theatre of Dionysus lies below as one looks down from the Acropolis. Much of the seating has disappeared, and various Hellenistic and Roman alterations have changed the layout of the stage buildings and the shape of the dancing circle. The representation on an Athenian coin is from the time of the Roman Empire. A line of figures under the stage, *above*, including the god Silenus also dates from the Roman period. The priest of Dionysus had the central decorated throne of honour in the auditorium, *right*

66 These bronze discs are the ancient Greek equivalent of theatre tickets. The letter indicated in which 'wedge' of the auditorium the ticket-holder was entitled to sit

prisoners were released on bail to attend; a meeting-point for visitors from the whole Hellenic world, to whom the city displayed the brilliance of her culture.

The requirements of the festival determined the nature of the place where it was held. As at a modern football match, there must be room for the entire public at a single performance; and this could only be achieved in daylight in the open air, on a site in or near the city suited by nature for the purpose. Structures of this kind could not easily be destroyed by either earthquakes or man, and we can still study the Theatre of Dionysus below the Acropolis at Athens as well as many others in the Greek and Roman world of which it was the prototype. But the remains at Athens share with most of the rest the defect that later alterations and additions confuse the picture; and as most of our other evidence on the subject also comes from later times, there are many doubtful points in our conception of the theatre in the days of Sophocles or Aristophanes.

The fifth-century theatre was a unified whole: all those present were participants in the festival. But they were divided into three sections, to which the three parts of the theatre correspond. The use of these in tragedy must be described first.

Ills 67, 69

The central feature was the *orchēstra*, the dancing-circle for the chorus. They were all men, twelve or fifteen in number, and wore masks and costumes representing their supposed sex and age and nationality and occupation. They marched on to the *orchēstra* after the opening scene of the play, and stayed until their departure brought it to an end. Their share in the performance took several forms: between the dialogue scenes they chanted choral songs to the accompaniment of a single flute; sometimes chorus and one or more actors sang in turn stanzas of lamentation or joy; their leader could intervene briefly in the dialogue; and in some plays they took part, though often an ineffective part, in the action itself. Of their movements we know little; but they certainly danced as they sang, and reacted with motions and gestures to the dialogue.

To the modern reader the utterances of the chorus often seem a tiresome interruption which he is tempted to skip, and to the modern producer they present a problem which he tries to solve in various ways – usually without success. Even during the fifth century their share of the play diminished, shrinking in some of the extant tragedies to a quarter or less. But their importance for the Athenian audience is evident: not only was their dancing-place the focal point in the theatre; in addition, a dramatic performance was usually called a *choros*, the parts of the play took their names from their relation to the chorus (thus *prologos*, the dialogue or speech spoken before the chorus enters); and many plays took their names from the chorus – *Suppliant Women, Trojan Women, Libation Bearers*, and other titles which seem colourless today. In two ways the existence of the chorus had a decisive effect on the nature of Greek tragedy. Their songs gave the action wider meaning by linking it with legend and tra-ditional belief. Their presence, far from breaking up the play, gave it unity – not necessarily unity of time or place, which was by no means always observed, but of action: a Greek tragedy was no chronicle play, but an organic and continuous whole.

Behind the *orchēstra*, as the audience saw it, and not as yet raised above it, was the area used by the actors, although they were free to mingle with the chorus on the dancing-circle itself. At their back the *skēnē*, originally a tent for changing in, was now a movable two-storey structure of wood normally representing a palace or temple, set perhaps above one or two broad steps, and with projecting side-wings at either end. With the help of scene-painting a variety of backgrounds – even sea-

Ill. 70

Ill. 68

67–69 The finest surviving example of an ancient Greek theatre is the one at Epidaurus in the Peloponnese, built in the fourth century BC. Its acoustics were famous in ancient times, and classical plays are still performed there today with the addition of modern stage settings (*left*). The dancing circle is still complete, with the base of an altar in the centre. The stone seating is sufficient for at least 17,000. The fragment *below* of a fourth century wine-jar from Tarentum shows actors on a stage set — a structure with columns, rich entablature and roof decorations

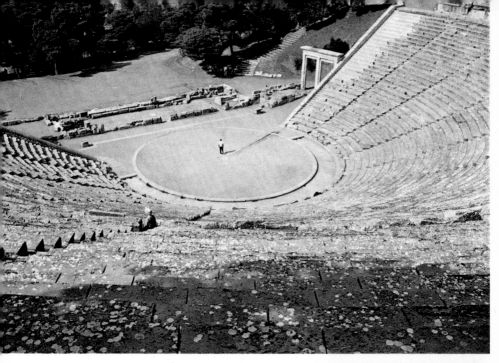

70, 71   In the late fourth-century vase-painting, *below*, a costumed actor holds his mask, which has natural features and slightly parted lips, unlike the distorted masks of later times. The terracotta figurine on the right shows an actor dressed for a female part

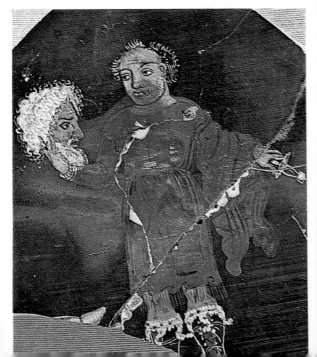

72 This detail from a fifth-century vase shows three actors carrying their masks. One of them seems to have the role of an oriental monarch; the others are probably taking part in a satyr-play

shore or a cave – could be shown. Like so much of Greek life, the action of the play took place in the open in front of the *skēnē*; events 'offstage', whether in the building which the *skēnē* represented or elsewhere, were reported by a messenger. Theatre devices included a crane (whereby gods could appear 'out of the machine') and a means of bringing within sight of the audience the result of violence indoors. The interior scenes so common in modern drama were impossible here, and no proscenium arch or other barrier separated audience from players.

Ill. 73

Ills 70, 72

Late representations of the tragic actor that have come down to us portray a grotesque masked figure with exaggerated forehead, gaping mouth, and boot soles several inches thick. The fifth century, however, knew nothing of these distortions: mask and costume then were not far removed from normal life, neither probably were gesture and movement, although the balance of

73 This melodramatic statuette probably represents a female character in tragedy (Clytemnestra?). It is Roman work of the second century A D, and the high forehead, wide-open eyes and mouth, and thick-soled shoes illustrate the exaggerated tragic costume of later times

74 In the sixth-century vase-painting, *below*, probably contemporary with the beginnings of drama, Dionysus (crowned with ivy) and a woman worshipper join with satyrs in a gay vintage scene. A play with a satyr chorus followed each trilogy of tragedies at Dionysus' festival

speech against speech and line against line in the dialogue has a ritual formality which may have been reflected in the acting. No doubt the actor's voice was the decisive factor in the competition for the prize for acting established in the middle of the century. Scarcity of men with good voices (there were no women actors) may have been the reason for using not more than three in each play, who with changes of mask and costumes shared the speaking parts between them. Silent 'extras' could be as numerous as finance allowed.

Alternation of dialogue and choral song was the fabric of each tragedy. Three from one poet were performed in succession, sometimes all on one theme, but more often as separate as three one-act plays; and they were followed by a short, boisterous, and amusing piece, still by the same author, with a chorus of satyrs led by the drunken Silenus. This was the fare presented to the ten judges and the thousands of citizens, visitors, women and children, even slaves, who gathered at daybreak on the wooden seating of the *theatron* ('watching-place'), the vast natural amphitheatre from which they looked down towards the dancing-circle at its foot. Seats of honour at the front were given to officials, priests, orphans of men killed in battle, and representatives of foreign States; but the shape of the site and the clear Greek air ensured that all could hear, except when hissing or applause or noisy consumption of food prevented it. Drama was a democratic occasion in the theatre at the foot of the Acropolis, which was to be the model for many others throughout the Greek world. Some of them were larger and more splendid, such as the magnificent fourth-century theatre, still much in use, at Epidaurus in the Peloponnese. But in essential character all followed the Athenian prototype until the disappearance of the chorus and purposes far removed from the drama of the fifth century modified their shape.

Ill. 71

Ill. 74

Ill. 75

Ills 62-65

Ills 67, 69

75　Vase-paintings do not show us the theatre audience. But some idea of the liveliness and excitement on the close-packed benches may be gained from this vivid picture of the funeral games of Patroclus on a fragment of a sixth-century mixing-bowl

The Origins of Tragedy

On the origin of this form of drama we have only scanty and conflicting evidence, and the controversies that have resulted from it are not likely to be resolved. What seems certain is that tragedy arose out of religious ritual, and that its oldest element is the part nearest to ritual – choral song. The lyric chorus narrated legend: at some time in the sixth century BC some poet – it may have been the Athenian, Thespis, about 534 – took the crucial step of introducing a *hypokrites*, an 'answerer' or 'interpreter' who could deliver speeches or converse with the leader of the chorus. Here was the first actor, bringing alive before the audience a character previously only described in narrative, adding a new dimension to that vivid presentation of individuals which pervades all Greek literature. With his advent, *drama* ('doing' the story, not merely telling it) was born; the name *tragōdia* ('goat-song'), is linked in some way with the importance of the goat in the worship of the fertility god Dionysus, in whose honour drama came to be performed.

How plays became an official part of the Great Dionysia, why three tragedies were performed together, why the satyr-play was added, are questions to which there is no certain answer. The development of these beginnings into drama in the full sense was largely the achievement of Aeschylus (525–456), whose introduction of a second actor made dialogue possible independent of the chorus. The use of a third actor, we are told, was initiated by Sophocles (496–406). During the fifth century hundreds of plays must have been presented by many different poets at the festivals of Dionysus, but all that now survives from this wealth of dramatic literature is a number of works by the three acknowledged masters of Attic tragedy, preserved through the centuries because they were thought suitable for study in the schools of Byzantium. Seven are by Aeschylus, including three that form the *Oresteia*, our only extant example of a trilogy on a single theme; another seven are by Sophocles; and seventeen are by Euripides (485–406). To these must be added the *Rhesus*, which some scholars see as an early work of Euripides, others as a fourth-century product; and also a satyr-play from Euripides and part of one from Sophocles.

The impact of recent discovery on our knowledge of Greek literature is illustrated by the problem of dating these plays. For the majority of them there is no external evidence of date, and where it is lacking apparent 'earliness' or 'lateness' is no reliable guide. Until a few years ago Aeschylus' *Suppliant Women* was judged by the predominance of the chorus and other 'primitive' features to be the first of his extant works, and placed as early as the first decade of the fifth century; but a reference on a scrap of papyrus discovered in Egypt shows that its date

Ill. 77

Ill. 76

76, 77   Euripides and Sophocles were nearly contemporary, and both died in the same year. The popularity of Euripides increased greatly after his death, and many busts of him are still extant, *left*. The bronze head of Sophocles, *right*, probably from the second century B C, may represent the poet in old age

was much later (probably 463) and that our earliest surviving Greek play is Aeschylus' *Persians*, produced in 472 when he was already fifty-four years old. If the evidence of the papyrus is accepted, we possess works only from Aeschylus' last years; and from Sophocles and Euripides also, as it happens, we have no complete play written before either was forty. This strange chance makes all the more tantalizing the efforts of scholars to piece together more knowledge of other plays by these and other playwrights from the many fragments already known or any new discoveries that come to light.

Legend in the Theatre

If we could read all fifth-century tragedy or a more representative cross-section, our conception of it might be far wider and more varied. Even what remains is enough to show that each of the three great tragic poets had his own approach to drama, his own way of handling plot and character. Yet thanks to tradition and the nature of the occasion and place of the performance of their plays, they had much in common. Occasionally, as in the *Persians*, they drew their themes from recent history. One of the earliest plays we hear of is *The Capture of Miletus*, in which Phrynichus dramatized the fall of the greatest city of Asiatic Greece to the Persians in 494 B C. Herodotus reports its reception:

> The whole theatre burst into tears, and the people sentenced him to pay a fine of a thousand drachmas, for recalling to them their own misfortunes. They likewise made a law, that no one should ever again exhibit that piece.

Normally, as was natural, playwrights sought their material from the same source to which choral poets had turned – the rich storehouse of myth and legend already available in epic poetry. Round about the end of the fifth century the experiment was tried of writing tragedies with newly invented plots and characters, as is usual for the modern stage, but the custom of using known stories persisted. What the audience expected of tragedy was to see the heroic figures of epic and hear them speak. With Shakespeare's histories or some plays of modern French dramatists in mind we can understand the Athenians' excitement over a fresh version of familiar material, or in judging the playwright's treatment of a common heritage. There was usually nothing openly topical in these plots drawn from the legendary past, as in *The Capture of Miletus*; but the dramatists, unlike Homer, often dealt by implication with burning issues of the day. It is difficult to read Euripides' portrayal of the pitiful aftermath of the fall of Troy in the *Trojan Women* (415 B C) without connecting it with the brutal Athenian conquest of the island of Melos in the previous year.

The handling of legend in the theatre was necessarily different in another way from its treatment in epic narrative. Most Greek tragedies presented only a climax – Agamemnon's return and death, Oedipus' discovery of the truth, Medea's revenge. Even a trilogy based on a single legend, like the *Oresteia*, did not present a continuous story, but three climaxes. The poet worked the climax on which his play was focused into dramatic form by devising a series of episodes, divided by choral songs, within this one phase of the legend, usually bringing the action to the highest dramatic pitch well before the end and closing on a quieter note. Reference was made to earlier and later events, but they were not portrayed or even narrated until Euripides adopted the practice of opening the play with an explanatory prologue and finishing it, in many cases, with a prophetic speech from a 'god out of the machine'. This concentration on a single climax is the cause of that unity of action to which Aristotle rightly points as the essential feature of Greek (or, as he supposes, of all) tragedy. The other unities of time and place which Renaissance commentators mistakenly found in his *Poetics* are not in his text, nor are they true of all the extant plays: in at least two there is a change of scene, and choral songs often cover long lapses of time. But unity of action is a quality rarely absent. Compared with such tightly compact plays as *Oedipus the King* much of Shakespeare is rambling and shapeless. Greek tragedy at its best is comparable with music in its enclosure of strong emotion within a well-ordered form.

A play constructed on this pattern leaves little room for development of character, and even elaboration in character-drawing is rare in Greek tragedy. Vigour in argument and intensity of feeling are the playwright's aim, not the psychological subtleties expected in the modern theatre. But the simplicity of the characters does not justify mechanical explanations of their actions or sufferings. The downfall of Oedipus or Ajax is not simply a punishment for a moral failing; a Greek tragedy is not just the working out of an ethical equation in which sin brings its own reward and right triumphs in the end. Nor are the characters to be regarded as mere puppets in the hands of fate or the gods, moving towards a pre-destined and inevitable doom. The 'infernal machine' of destiny controls every step in Cocteau's dramatization of the Oedipus legend, but this is not Sophocles' conception of the story; if it were, his *Oedipus the King* would be a much inferior play. Both poetic justice and fate were important elements in fifth-century drama, but neither of them prevented playwright or audience from seeing the characters as free individuals acting according to their own choice. The impossibility of believing in both pre-destination and freewill remained as yet unrecognized, as it had been by Homer and still is by most people today; and although this may have been bad philosophy, it made good drama. Just because the figures of legend were seen not as cogs in a machine but as individuals with minds and wills of their own, there was great freedom and variety in depicting them. The most familiar, Odysseus or Clytemnestra or Heracles, could be very different in different plays, even where the author was the same; and many of the lowly characters without a name – mes-sengers, nurses, watchmen – are as distinct and memor-able as their Shakespearian equivalents, although they use the same metre and practically the same language as the great.

The use of traditional material did not prevent almost equal diversity of plot. Unrestricted by religious dogma, Greek legend admitted endless variation, and the poet could select a well-known or little-known version as he chose and make his own alterations and additions. The essentials of the most familiar stories were fixed: Orestes must kill Clytemnestra, not be reconciled with her. But

78 The suicide of the Greek warrior Ajax, disappointed in the contest for the arms of the dead Achilles, is the subject of one of the seven surviving tragedies of Sophocles. This bronze statuette from an Etruscan city is probably of about the same date

within these bare outlines there was always scope for originality of invention, and without wearying the audience many dramatists could ring the changes on a single theme. Their treatment of it was not limited by any narrow conception of 'tragedy' such as we derive from Aristotle: the examples that we possess include a number which have a happy ending, and their mood ranges from the horror of Sophocles' *Oedipus the King* to the romantic comedy of Euripides' *Helen*. The audience found plenty to surprise it in each poet's new handling of a traditional tale.

Three Plays of Orestes and Electra

Three of the extant plays provide an opportunity of studying a particular example of this variety and the different approaches of the three tragedians: their treatment of the revenge of Orestes, dramatized by Aeschylus in the *Libation-Bearers*, second play of the *Oresteia* trilogy, in 458 BC, and forty or more years later by Sophocles and Euripides in two plays both entitled *Electra*. The

Ills 79, 80 story of the murder of Agamemnon on his return from Troy by Clytemnestra and her lover, Aegisthus, and of the penalty which Orestes later exacted from them, was one of the most familiar of heroic legends. It is related briefly in the *Odyssey*, where Orestes' vengeance is represented as a righteous act of retribution against Aegisthus: the manner of Clytemnestra's death is not told. It reappeared in the 'Epic Cycle', and was the subject of a long lyric poem by Stesichorus: in his version Orestes seems to have killed both Clytemnestra and Aegisthus in obedience to Apollo, who protected him with his bow

Ill. 87 when the Furies, goddesses who punished unnatural crime, persecuted him for the matricide. The same theme, again variously handled, is to be found in fifth-century art.

Aeschylus is said to have described his plays as 'slices from the great banquets of Homer', but his treatment of

Ills 81, 82 the legend in the *Oresteia* is not Homeric. Deeply concerned with its moral and religious aspect, he portrays it as a story of murder and counter-murder within the family, choosing for the three plays of his trilogy three focal points: the death of Agamemnon, Orestes' revenge, and (perhaps his own invention) the end of the sequence through Orestes' trial and acquittal before an Athenian court. Like Stesichorus, he makes Apollo responsible for Orestes' act, and to suit his interpretation his emphasis

Ills 83-86 naturally falls on Clytemnestra rather than Aegisthus. She is the central figure of the first play, the *Agamemnon*. In the *Libation-Bearers*, after Orestes and his friend Pylades have revealed themselves to Electra and the chorus of women and joined them in lengthy ritual at Agamemnon's tomb, the killing of Aegisthus within the palace is only a prelude to the dramatic and moral climax – the clash between Clytemnestra and her son and her

82

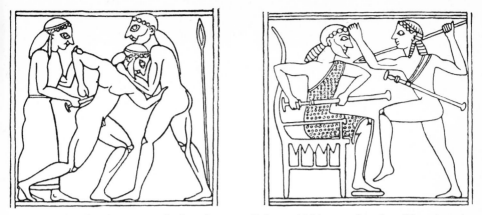

79, 80 These drawings are made from bronze reliefs on shield-straps found at Olympia – the earliest surviving representations of the murder of Agamemnon and the killing of Aegisthus. Both are more than a century earlier than Aeschylus' dramatization of the story in the *Oresteia*

pleas for mercy, rejected when Pylades reminds Orestes of Apollo's command:

CLYTEMNESTRA Down with your sword, my son! My own child, see this breast:
Here often your head lay, in sleep, while your soft mouth
Sucked from me the good milk that gave you life and strength.
ORESTES Pylades, what shall I do? To kill a mother is terrible,
Shall I show mercy?
PYLADES Where then are Apollo's words,
His Pythian oracles? What becomes of men's sworn oaths?
Make all men living your enemies, but not the gods.
ORESTES I uphold your judgment; your advice is good.
(*To Clyt.*) Come on;
I mean to kill you close beside him. While he lived
You preferred him to my father. Sleep with him in death.

Soon Orestes drives her into the palace. But his revenge is quickly followed by the approach of the Furies, and at

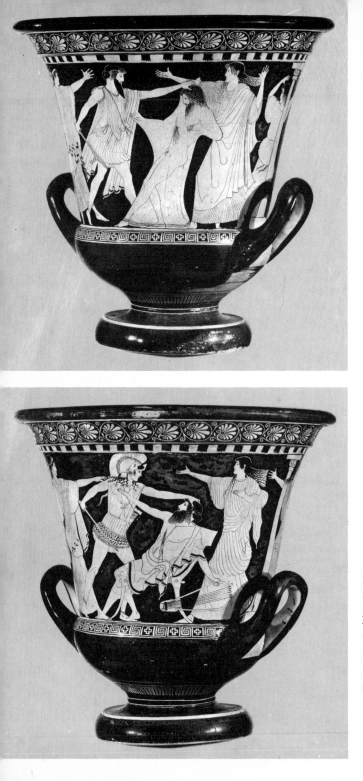

81, 82 The fine paintings on the two sides of the wine-bowl on the left are so closely related to Aeschylus' *Oresteia* that they probably date from the same year (458 BC) or very soon afterwards. On one side, *above*, Agamemnon, trapped in a net, sinks to the ground with blood flowing from his breast, faced by Aegisthus with a sword and Clytemnestra with an axe. Behind him Electra flings out an arm in protest and another woman (Chrysothemis?) runs off in horror. On the other side, *left*, the tables are turned: Aegisthus, with Electra behind him, is killed by Orestes while Clytemnestra fails to hold the avenger back

83–86 The story of Agamemnon's murder and Orestes' revenge was a favourite with the vase-painters as well as the dramatists. *Left above*, Clytemnestra runs with double-axe towards a great palace door: she must be running to save Aegisthus – but actually to her own death. *Right*, she kills the Trojan princess Cassandra, whom Agamemnon had brought back with him from the war. *Below*, the two faces of an early fifth-century vase picture Orestes' revenge in a way perhaps taken from a wall-painting in Athens. The queen again carries her axe, but is prevented from intervening while Aegisthus is killed

the end of the play he is no righteous hero, but a hunted man. The rights and wrongs remain to be debated by Apollo and the Furies before Athena and her jurymen.

Sophocles also, as his *Antigone* shows, was far from blind to moral and religious issues. But the outstanding features of his *Electra* are his portrait of the heroine and, above all, that mastery of plot-construction in which Aristotle found him pre-eminent. His play stood by itself without prelude or sequel, and for it he constructed a version of the story close to the *Odyssey*. The recognition between brother and sister is managed with much greater skill than in the *Oresteia*, and the revenge involves a *coup de théâtre* such as Aeschylus never achieves. Orestes and Pylades gain entrance to the palace by posing as strangers bringing a report of Orestes' death and bearing his ashes. There they kill Clytemnestra. Aegisthus, away when they arrived and returning in haste at their news, is confronted with the sight of the two 'strangers' standing beside a covered body – as he supposes, the corpse of Orestes. After a moment of pretended grief he speaks to Electra, as he approaches to uncover the body:

> AEGISTHUS Call Clytemnestra here,
>   If she is in the house.
> ORESTES She is near you now,
>   Not far to seek.
> AEGISTHUS (*lifting the covering*)
>   God, what is this?
> ORESTES Afraid? Of whom? Strangers?
> AEGISTHUS Whose trap is this
>   That I have fallen into?
> ORESTES Are you so blind
>   You cannot tell the living from the dead?

Not only the order of events has changed from Aeschylus' version. The dramatic emphasis has reverted to Aegisthus, and the evaluation of the story to the Homeric point of

87 To escape from the Furies Orestes took refuge at Delphi. On this fourth-century vase he clings for sanctuary to the stone there known as the *omphalos* or navel, the reputed centre of the earth. Apollo warns off a flying Fury while a priestess runs away. On the right is Artemis

view. 'This day's work is well done', sing the chorus as they go off when Aegisthus has been taken into the palace. Of the Furies no mention is made.

In Euripides' *Electra*, probably produced after Sophocles' play and intended as a reply to it, we are again far from Homer. Here as in many of his plays he stripped away the glamour from legend, criticized the alleged behaviour of the gods, and set the heroic characters in a new and often sordid light – realistic trends which won him little popularity in his day but made him the favourite dramatist of subsequent generations, the main link with both later tragedy and the comedy of manners. His Electra is living in poverty, married to a peasant, whose cottage forms the background to the action. The order of events is as in Aeschylus: Aegisthus is the first victim, and the climax is the killing of Clytemnestra, for which the wavering Orestes is steeled not by any reminder of Apollo's will, but by his sister's ferocious determination. The sequel to the murder is not the onslaught of the Furies, but a song in which the two describe to the chorus the horror of what they have done – the kind of scene which prompted Aristotle to call Euripides 'the most tragic of the poets':

ORESTES Did you see how, in her agony,
　　　She opened her gown, thrust forth her breast,
　　　And showed it to me as I struck?
　　　Her body that gave me birth
　　　Sprawled there on the ground.
　　　I had her by the hair . . .
CHORUS I know what torture you went through;
　　　I heard her shriek – your own mother.
ELECTRA Yes; as she uttered that shriek
　　　She was putting her hand on my face;
　　　'My child, I implore you,' she said.
　　　Then she hung around my neck
　　　So that the sword fell out of my hand.
CHORUS Wretched, miserable woman! How could you
　　　　　　　　　　　　　　　　　　　　bear
　　　To see with your own eyes
　　　Your mother gasping out her life?
ORESTES I held my cloak over my eyes,
　　　While with my sword I performed sacrifice,
　　　Driving the blade into my mother's throat.

This play, like others of Euripides, is ended by intervention from Heaven. Clytemnestra's divine twin brothers, Castor and Pollux, appear 'out of the machine' and foretell the future, laying the blame for Orestes' act squarely on the 'unwise utterances' of Apollo. Electra is to marry Pylades, Orestes to escape the Furies by standing trial at Athens. Here Euripides echoes Aeschylus;

yet five years later, in the *Orestes*, he devised a different sequel to the revenge – a melodrama in which brother and sister, still in Argos, go from crime to crime in their desperate efforts to escape execution by the people. Freedom in remoulding and reinterpreting legend, which has given many different versions of the Orestes story to more modern literature, was the accepted practice and one of the main attractions for the audience in the theatre of Dionysus.

The Birth of Comedy

Comedy was presented at Athens at the same festivals as tragedy. Each competing poet put on one play, approximately equal to a tragedy in length and similarly divided between a chorus (twenty-four, often split into two groups) and three male actors who performed all the speaking parts. What little evidence we have of the origins of comedy suggests that like tragedy it came into *Ills 90, 91* being through the addition of dialogue to choral song: acted episodes, imitated perhaps from Peloponnesian models, may have been combined in Attica with the festive singing and dancing of a *kōmos* ('chorus of revellers') which originated in fertility ritual and gave *kōmōdia* ('song of the *kōmos*') its name.

To this extent the great branches of drama followed the same general pattern, but here the resemblance ends. When we turn from tragedy to the eleven extant plays of Aristophanes – the only complete fifth-century or early fourth-century comedies that we now possess – we move from high to low: the spectator watching the comic actor play Trygaeus, the grape-farmer, or the old peasant Strepsiades, no longer had before him one of the heroic beings of legend, but a grotesque caricature of his own unheroic self – a ludicrous figure with distorted mask, *Ills 88, 89* padded belly and buttocks, and a large artificial phallus. In keeping with this costume the language of the dialogue

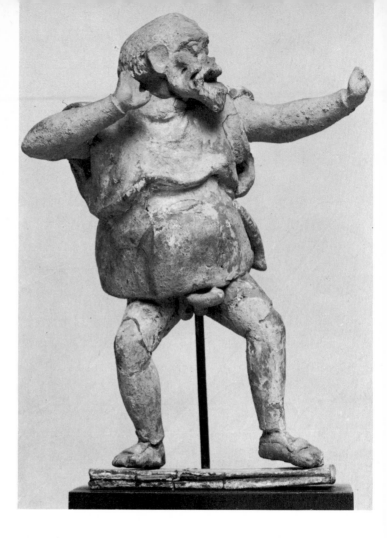

was full of frank obscenity, a feature of ordinary life often reflected in vase paintings, but not normally in literature. The time represented was not the mythical past but the present: Aristophanic comedy struck a contemporary note, and its satire was always topical. Along with the Athenian equivalent of John Citizen, other actors, wearing portrait-masks, would caricature with unparalleled freedom the leading personalities of the day – Socrates, the highbrow crank, Euripides, the degenerate intellectual, Cleon, the arrogant demagogue. A fragment of

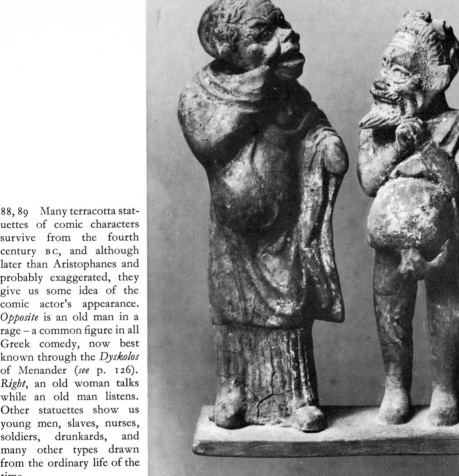

88, 89 Many terracotta statuettes of comic characters survive from the fourth century BC, and although later than Aristophanes and probably exaggerated, they give us some idea of the comic actor's appearance. *Opposite* is an old man in a rage – a common figure in all Greek comedy, now best known through the *Dyskolos* of Menander (*see* p. 126). *Right*, an old woman talks while an old man listens. Other statuettes show us young men, slaves, nurses, soldiers, drunkards, and many other types drawn from the ordinary life of the time

Cratinus, earlier than Aristophanes, shows that even 'Olympian' Pericles was included in the rogues' gallery of the comic playwrights. The actor representing him evidently entered wearing on his head a model of the latest much-criticized addition to the Athenian building programme, the Odeum; and another exclaimed:

Here's Pericles, our own squill-headed Zeus.
    Where *did* he buy that hat? With what excuse?
It's new head-cover in Odeum style –
    Late storms of censure hardly left a Tile.

Topical comment could come from the chorus as well as in the dialogue. The play could be interrupted by a section in which they came forward and put directly to the audience the poet's views on current affairs. Comedy was surely the most typical literary product of democratic Athens.

In these ways comedy brought drama down to earth. But it also lifted it skywards in amazing flights of poetry and fantasy. Few things in Greek literature surpass the beauty of some of Aristophanes' choral songs; and no other author can compare with the soaring imagination of the extravaganzas which he built out of the emotional trends of the day: out of the growing desire for peace during the Peloponnesian War, the picture of farmer Dikaiopolis making a one-man truce with Sparta (*Acharn-*

90, 91 These masks of bronze (*left*) and terracotta (*right*), both from the Hellenistic period, symbolize the contrast between tragedy and comedy – a division begun by the Greeks and maintained throughout antiquity, although both branches of drama probably had their origins in the worship of the same god, Dionysus

ians, 425 BC), or of Trygaeus flying to heaven in search of Peace on a dung-beetle (*Peace*, 421), or of Lysistrata leading the women in a sex strike which brings the men to their senses (*Lysistrata*, 411); out of the weariness which spread as the war dragged on, the conception of a Utopian 'Cloud-Cuckoo-Town' built by the birds in the sky (*Birds*, 414); out of the post-war hardships, a burlesque of the welfare state (*Women in Parliament*, 391).

The antics and adventures of Aristophanes' 'little men' in these extraordinary situations provide most of the fun of the comedies, but he reaches the greatest heights of poetic fantasy in his handling of the chorus. Vase paintings show that the dancing chorus masquerading as animals or birds may go back to Mycenaean times: Aristophanes uses it with spectacular effect in his *Wasps*

Ills 92-94
Ill. 95

93

92, 93 Long before Aristophanes vase-paintings portray dancing choruses, led by a flute-player, with animal or bird costumes and masks, although we can only guess at the ritual occasion which they depict. On the left are men dressed as cocks. The masquerade of men on horse-back on the sixth-century vase, *opposite*, anticipates the chorus of Aristophanes' comedy, *The Knights*, which won the first prize in 424 BC. In other plays by him there are choruses of wasps, birds, frogs and even clouds

and *Clouds* and above all in the *Birds*, where each bird has his own distinctive costume and call. Little wonder that in their address to the audience they claim that comedy is more entertaining than tragedy:

Truly to be clad in feathers is the very best of things.
Only fancy, dear spectators, had you each a brace of wings,
Never need you, tired and hungry, at a Tragic Chorus stay,
You would likely, when it bored you, spread your wings and fly away,
Back returning, after luncheon, to enjoy our Comic Play.

A Mission to Hades

Not only his contemporaries were targets for Aristophanes' satire and fantasy. Other regular victims were the heroes of legend, tragedy, mercilessly parodied, and – by

no means least – the gods. In the *Frogs*, presented in the year after the death of Sophocles and Euripides, Dionysus himself becomes a figure of fun. The date is 405 BC, and the long war against Sparta is nearing its grim conclusion. In the atmosphere of accumulating disaster and impending defeat for Athens, Aristophanes keeps away from the subject of politics, except for a brief warning when the chorus speaks directly to the audience; instead he turns to the future of poetry, and writes a play which incidentally tells us a great deal about the Athenian citizen's attitude to tragedy.

As the city now has no great living tragic poet, her only hope lies in bringing one back from the dead; and who could be better fitted for the errand than the god of drama himself? One of the Labours of Heracles was a visit to Hades to kidnap the monstrous dog Cerberus; so Dionysus disguises himself as Heracles, with lion-skin and club added to the long robe and high boots of

Ill. 96

tragedy, and goes on his journey accompanied (of course) by a slave and a donkey. As they approach the Underworld the donkey disappears, and in a typical Aristophanic moment they try to persuade a passing funeral to take their baggage for them. In a lively modern prose translation:

DIONYSUS Er – hullo, excuse me! Yes, you there! Stiff! (*The litter-bearers come to a halt. The corpse sits up with a jerk.*)
Ah, would you do me a favour and take my baggage to blazes?
CORPSE How many pieces?
DIONYSUS Just these.
CORPSE That'll be two drachmas.
DIONYSUS Too much.
CORPSE Bearers, proceed!
DIONYSUS Hi, wait a minute! Can't we come to some arrangement?
CORPSE Two drachmas, cash down, or nothing.
DIONYSUS (*counting out his small change*) I can pay you nine obols.
CORPSE I'd sooner live!

Presently they reach the Styx, and while the slave 'walks round' ferryman Charon makes Dionysus row across, speeded on by the unseen chorus of frogs which gives the play its name:

> Brekeke-kex, ko-ax, ko-ax,
> Ko-ax, ko-ax, ko-ax,
> Oh we are the musical Frogs!
> We live in the marshes and bogs!
> Sweet, sweet is the hymn
> That we sing as we swim . . .

After passing through one ridiculous scrape after another master and slave eventually reach the house of Pluto, where Dionysus is called on to decide the claim of the lately arrived Euripides to replace Aeschylus on the throne of tragedy (Sophocles, also a newcomer, is conveniently kept out of the picture). With typical disregard for consistency the caricature of the god now becomes a portrait of the man-in-the-street or the man-in-the-audience, baffled by both contestants yet judging them by definite standards among which morality and craftsmanship are assumed to matter most:

AESCHYLUS What are the qualities that you look for in a good poet?

EURIPIDES Technical skill – and he should teach a lesson, make people into better citizens.

AESCHYLUS And if you have failed to do this? If you have presented good men, noble men, as despicable wretches, what punishment do you think you deserve?

DIONYSUS Death. No good asking him.

In the argument that follows questions of technical skill bulk surprisingly large: jokes based on metrical points remind us how much the *sound* of poetry must have mattered to an audience which depended on the ear rather than the written word. In the end Dionysus chooses Aeschylus. Many modern readers would agree with him, although not for the same reasons; but his verdict was not that of later antiquity: in the fourth century and in later Greek and Roman times Euripides became the most popular of the three tragedians and exercised most influence on the development of drama.

The *Frogs* is a healthy corrective to exaggerated estimates of the intellectual level of the Athenian public; but it fully confirms the existence among the great audience in the theatre of Dionysus of that lively and critical interest in drama which was the background to the brilliant achievements of the fifth century in tragedy and comedy alike.

97

96   In Aristophanes' *Frogs*, Dionysus descends to Hades disguised as Heracles, who as one of
is labours was sent to the underworld by Eurystheus to kidnap the three-headed dog Cerberus.
n this lively vase-painting Heracles has brought Cerberus back and shows him to Eurystheus,
who takes refuge in a jar

94, 95   In one of the finest of Aristophanes' comedies a chorus of birds, each with its distinctive
ostume, build a 'Cloud-Cuckoo-Town' in the sky. The vase-painting of dancers dressed as birds
ates from nearly a century earlier. The fresco fragment, *below*, is from Mycenae and suggests
hat ritual animal masquerade goes back to Mycenaean times

CHAPTER FOUR

The Rise of Prose

The Beginnings

By the end of the fifth century B C a rich variety of verse
forms – epic, tragedy, comedy, all the different types of
individual and choral song – had arisen in Greece and
reached maturity and produced their most brilliant
results. The Greeks far surpassed their older neighbours
of the Near East in the attention they devoted to poetry
and in their poetic achievement. But what of prose?

If 'prose' means merely the use of words in non-
metrical sequence, presumably it was as old as the Greek
language itself – spoken in the course of ordinary talk,
used in written records whether in Linear B or alphabetic
script. Our concern, however, is with the rise of non-
metrical speech or writing to a level of artistry at which
it could reasonably be called 'literature'. The early phases
of the story are little less obscure than the origins of epic
or drama: in prose, as in verse, the works now extant are
products of maturity, when growing pains were past. The
earliest prose book which we possess complete is the
History of Herodotus from the mid-fifth century, and
from the many earlier writers no more than scraps survive. All that can be done is to supply some background
to the three main types of prose literature that flourished
in the fifth and fourth centuries – history, oratory, and
the philosophic dialogue.

97 Aesop with the fox which figures so often in his fables. He is said to have been a slave on the island of Samos in the sixth century BC

Several elements contributed to the making of history: the practice in some cities, for example, of keeping local records and lists; popular non-verse telling of traditional tales, of which the fables attributed to Aesop, known to us only in much later form, may have been an example. But the driving force which eventually produced Herodotus and Thucydides came less from tradition than from revolt against it. The word *historiē* means inquiry or the results of inquiry – search for truth as opposed to tradition, fact as opposed to fiction; and because tradition and fiction were normally expressed in verse, the new radical spirit of *historiē* which came to the fore in Ionia in the sixth century BC readily adopted prose as its medium. Inquiry might be pursued in various fields. Some looked for a more rational explanation of the universe, like Anaximander, who is said to have written one of the earliest books in prose. Others, like Hecataeus, travelled widely in foreign lands and described in prose what they had seen or heard. The opening sentences of one of Hecataeus' works happen to have reached us:

Ill. 97

101

Thus speaks Hecataeus of Miletus. What follows I write as it appears to me to be true; for the writings of the Greeks are many and in my opinion ridiculous.

These simple and abrupt statements contain the essentials of the new spirit that gave prose an independent status: the strong assertion of individual opinion; the emphasis on truth; the contemptuous rejection of 'the writings of the Greeks' by one who has seen the wonders of Egypt and the East.

It must not be supposed, of course, that all new attitudes or new ideas were expressed in prose. The verses of the radical thinker Xenophanes have already been quoted, and others – Parmenides, for example, and Empedocles – put forward their new theories in hexameters. Even contemporary history could still be presented in epic form. Nevertheless, in the course of the fifth century prose became established as the medium for conveying information or publishing results of *historiē* which the writer championed against older views. It was in prose that Anaxagoras published at Athens the heretical views about the sun and the moon which caused his exile, and in prose that Democritus set forth his atomic theory. Some of the most extensive remains of fifth-century writing, vitally important for the history of science but only occasionally worth consideration as literature, are prose treatises in the large collection found by third-century scholars on the island of Cos and attributed to Hippocrates, though how many are really his work we cannot know. The spirit of *historiē* is nowhere stronger than in the Hippocratic discussions of the true nature of the human body, the effect of climate on natural character, or the real explanation – epilepsy – of the disease traditionally known as 'sacred'. Prose is the natural and inevitable vehicle here: one cannot imagine Hippocrates or his colleagues writing in verse.

Ill. 98

98 This great plane tree on the island of Cos is alleged to be the one under which Hippocrates taught in the fifth century BC. The 'Hippocratic Oath' included among the writings ascribed to him still provides a code of conduct for doctors today

The 'Father of History'

The creation of history, in something like the modern sense of the word, out of *historiē* was the achievement of Herodotus. Born at Halicarnassus early in the fifth century, Herodotus later lived at Athens and joined the Athenian colony of Thurii in southern Italy; but much of his life was spent in travelling still more widely over the Greek and non-Greek world. Many of the five hundred pages of his book present (along with material drawn from earlier writings) the harvest of information which he gathered on his travels: one long section takes us to Egypt, others to Thrace, Scythia, North Africa, India, Babylon. What distinguishes Herodotus from his predecessors is the inclusion of all this within a single historical framework – the narrative of the struggle

Ill. 99

Ills 105, 106

99–102 The central theme of the History of Herodotus (*left*) is the Greek struggle against Persia and the events which led up to it, although he includes information gathered on his extensive travels about most of the world known to the Greeks in his day. Vase-paintings illustrate his story. *Below left*, the Persian king Darius is seen listening to a messenger, perhaps before setting out on the great invasion. *Below right*, Croesus king of Lydia, overthrown by the Persians, is placed on a pyre (he was saved when Apollo sent a rainstorm to extinguish the flames). *Opposite*, an amphora contemporary with the Persian Wars shows a Greek soldier spearing a Persian bowman

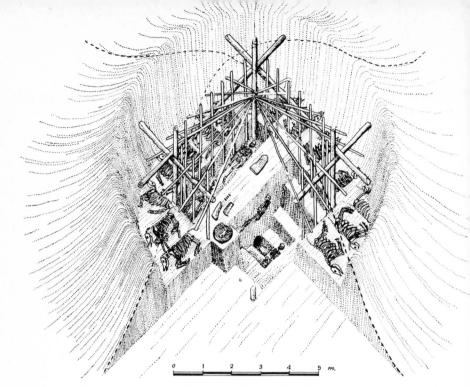

103, 104 Herodotus' remarkable description of Scythian burial customs has been dramatically confirmed by discoveries in Russia. The reconstruction above shows the sixth-century BC royal tomb at Kostromskaya: the chief was found buried in a subterranean chamber, while above and around lay thirteen skeletons of sacrificed human victims and eleven pairs of skeletons of sacrificed horses, all beneath a great earthen mound. The body *below* was found in a Siberian barrow the contents of which, frozen in ice, had altered little in more than twenty-three centuries. The corpse had been embalmed by a process which Herodotus describes

105, 106   This Greek-made vase from South Russia gives a first-hand picture of Scythians which agrees with Herodotus' account. They wear caps, short belted tunics, and trousers tucked into soft boots. After a battle one warrior restrings his bow, another has a wound dressed by a comrade

between Greece and Persia, which is stated as the book's subject in its opening sentence, provides a connecting chain through two-thirds of its length, and culminates in a narrative of Persian aggression and its defeat that sweeps majestically forward almost without a break. Whether this historical pattern was in the author's mind from the first or a structure superimposed later, is a much-disputed question. The result, however it came about, is a work of epic dimensions, embodying a magnificently broad conception of history. Yet for all his breadth of view Herodotus is never abstract: he is always concerned with particular places and events, particular customs and beliefs; above all, his pages are a portrait gallery of famous men and women, although the hero of his narrative as a whole is Athens itself.

Herodotus has a childlike love of marvels – Indian ants bigger than foxes, the gruesome burial ceremonies of Scythian kings – and he describes them in a story-telling

Ills 100-102

Ills 103, 104

style so apparently simple that its art passes unnoticed. He is too easily regarded as a mere narrator of wonders. In reality his outlook is the insatiable questioning spirit of *historië*, seeking truth and repeatedly giving voice to doubt. Of the diver who was said to have escaped from the Persians by staying beneath the surface of the sea for nearly ten miles, he writes:

> How he did reach the Greeks I cannot say with certainty, but I should be surprised if the story told is true. . . . My own opinion is that he came to Artemisium in a boat.

The 'father of history', as he is rightly called, is no credulous fool. He is often sceptical. But he has been rightly called an 'inquiring amateur', for he has no expert knowledge of any aspect of his subject and is quite unsystematic in his treatment of evidence. He accepts as 'the real facts' the Egyptians' story of their reason for regarding the Phrygians as the oldest race – that when two children were isolated from birth from all human speech, the first word they uttered was the Phrygian name for bread. Yet lack of confirmation by an eye-witness makes him doubt whether 'there is any sea on the further side of Europe', and in describing the first Phoenician voyage round Africa he refuses to believe the very feature of their report which indicates its truth – that as they travelled round from east to west 'they had the sun on their right hand'. History for Herodotus is certainly an art, not a science. For a more scientific approach, and the first statement of principles acceptable to a modern historian, we must turn to his young contemporary, Thucydides.

Ill. 107

The First Scientific Historian

Athenian born and bred, Thucydides had reached the position of general by 424 BC, when he was held responsible for a defeat and exiled. For twenty years, till he

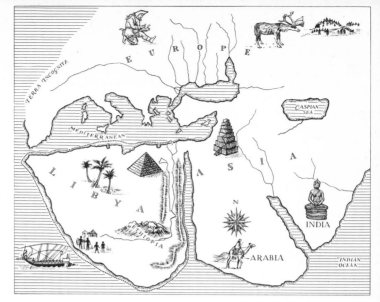

107 The world as it was probably conceived by Herodotus. His account of it is often surprisingly correct. The route round Africa of the Phoenician sailors whose voyage he describes is shown by a dotted line

returned to Athens shortly before his death, circumstances placed him, like Herodotus, in the position of an observer. His choice was to concentrate his attention on contemporary history: his work begins with a survey of the past, but only to demonstrate 'the feebleness of antiquity' and the unprecedented size and importance of the struggle between Athens and Sparta. The rest, with few digressions, describes the course of the Peloponnesian War down to 411, where it breaks off, unfinished and unrevised.

How far the book was constructed on a single plan, we do not know; but it bears all the marks of a rational and systematic approach to the writing of history. In contrast with Herodotus' breadth of view, Thucydides restricts his theme to the military events of the war and the reasons for them. He adopts a simple summer-winter division of each year to avoid chronological confusion. He handles evidence in accordance with rules comparable with the precision of medical science at the time:

With regard to my factual reporting of the events of the war I have made it a principle not to write down the first story that came my way, and not even to be

guided by my own general impressions; either I was present myself at the events which I have described or else I heard of them from eye-witnesses whose reports I have checked with as much thoroughness as possible.

The *History* of Herodotus, like Homeric epic, included speeches by leading characters in the narrative: this practice also Thucydides systematized and adapted to his own ends, putting into the mouths of the speakers the motives which prompted an action, the arguments for and against it, the policies and principles involved. His work is a book of permanent value meant for study, not (and here, no doubt, his implied attack is directed against Herodotus) a romantic story intended to please an audience:

It may well be that my history will seem less easy to read because of the absence in it of a romantic element. It will be enough for me, however, if these words of mine are judged useful by those who want to understand clearly the events which happened in the past and which (human nature being what it is) will, at some time or other and in much the same ways, be repeated in the future. My work is not a piece of writing designed to meet the taste of an immediate public, but was done to last for ever.

Thucydides' proud claim to immortality has proved correct: his book is still absorbing reading, but not only because of its scientific approach to history. It has other qualities which make it great literature. His swift narrative has a unique and paradoxical style: it breathes the spirit of contemporary rationalism yet has an old-fashioned flavour; it is concise and austere, yet forceful and impassioned. The style is typical of the man. By no means impartial, he is deeply committed to support of Pericles and his policy, deeply moved by Athens' folly (as he sees it) and its disastrous results; yet he austerely surveys the whole story as a clinical example of human

Ill. 108

behaviour under the stresses of imperialism and war. In Thucydides' account of the tragedy of Athens there is a grandeur of conception, as well as an intensity of feeling, which would have stood out even more clearly if he had been able to continue the story to the end.

Thucydides had no successor. The fourth century, mainly a century of prose, was not lacking in historians, but produced none comparable with the giants of the fifth. The only one of them whose writings are now extant is Xenophon (*c.* 430–354), who has considerable charm but little intellectual power: his *Hellenica*, in which he completes Thucydides' unfinished narrative of the Peloponnesian War and continues down to 362 B C, shows that he has neither his predecessor's insight nor his grasp of scientific principles. But his works may at any rate be a better mirror of his times than the creations of more brilliant minds. One trend reflected in them is a movement towards biography, exemplified in memoirs of Socrates and idealized accounts of Cyrus, founder of the Persian Empire, and the Spartan king Agesilaus; and much the most readable product of Xenophon's pen is auto-biographical – the *Anabasis* or *March Inland*, a simple but vivid narrative of the adventures of the ten thousand or more Greeks who joined an expedition to attack Babylon in 401, and after its failure struggled back to Greece under Xenophon's leadership.

The Prose of Persuasion

Xenophon is largely free from the influence which dominated most historical writing from the fourth century onwards: the influence of rhetoric, by nature inimical to the spirit of the early historians, although Thucydides was considerably affected by it. The object of *historiē* was to discover the truth; rhetoric was concerned with *persuasion*, a process in which eloquence was all-important and truth could go to the wall. The rise of rhetoric, first in Sicily and then at Athens, in the fifth century, and its growing importance thereafter in Greek life and education and literature, are phenomena which need not surprise us in a society still far more dependent on the spoken than the written word, which now developed political forms that made oratory the highroad to success: government by mass meeting and trial by mass jury put a premium on the art of effective speech, and teachers of it – the Sophists – became familiar figures in Athens and other cities by the time of the Peloponnesian War.

The Sophists were not primarily writers, and little that they wrote has survived. Our evidence about them comes mainly from Plato and other hostile sources, and it is not easy to judge their importance in the history of either thought or literature. But one point on which there can be no doubt is that among them we find for the first time deliberate study of the function of words and the technique of using them – the basis for development of the treatment of speech or writing as a conscious art. Protagoras, the first to call himself a Sophist, made a beginning of grammatical analysis. Prodicus' differentiation of synonyms is parodied by Plato, but was an important step forward. Gorgias, from Sicily, tried to enrich prose with poetical words and phrases, and worked out rhetorical devices – antithesis, balanced rhythm, assonance, even rhyme – which he was the first to call 'figures of speech'. Some idea of the highly artificial results of this first conscious cultivation of prose style can be gained from literal translation of part of a fragment of Gorgias himself, taken from a funeral speech for soldiers killed in war:

What qualities did these men lack of those that men should possess? And what did they possess that men should not possess? May I be able to say what I wish and may I wish what I should, escaping the vengeance of the gods, avoiding the envy of men. For divine was the courage these men possessed, but human their mortality. . . .

Such language (still more artificial in the original Greek) is reminiscent of the parody of Euphuism which Shakespeare puts into the mouth of Falstaff: 'Now I do not speak to thee in drink but in tears; not in pleasure but in passion; not in words only but in woes also.' Carried to extremes, such highly contrived use of word patterns easily became ridiculous and could not last; but from now onwards conscious artistry coloured most Greek prose – oratory, of course, above all. The influence of Gorgias is evident in the speeches which Thucydides attributes to political leaders. But it was in the next century that the art of eloquence reached maturity and its greatest heights.

The fourth century has bequeathed to us a large number of speeches by Attic orators. Many are law-court addresses, more emotional and more slanderous than those of today, and often inspired by political motives. Others are orations delivered in the Assembly, readable now only if we can recapture some of the sense of controversy or crisis which excited the original audience. A few belong to the category of public lectures, designed for great occasions such as the games at Olympia. Among their authors are Andocides, high-born gentleman and amateur in the practice of rhetoric; Lysias, skilful advocate and professional writer of speeches for others, with a style full of deliberate art for all its apparent simplicity; Isaeus, specialist on the law of inheritance; Lycurgus, diehard patriotic opponent of Macedon; and Aeschines, a tragic actor before he turned his wits to political opportunism. But critics ancient and modern agree that the greatest master of eloquence, in political and law-court speeches alike, is Demosthenes (384–322), whose passionate warnings against the threat to Greek freedom

109 Demosthenes of Athens, the greatest of Greek orators, was the eloquent advocate of a militant policy against the increasing power of Macedon

have had many echoes in the modern world. There is
remarkable variety of both style and matter in Demosthenes' many surviving works. As circumstances demand
he can be simple in language or grandiose, address the
Assembly in terms of high principle or resort to violent
personal invective to entertain a jury. Two brief extracts
from his famous speech *On the Crown* (330), in which he
defends his own past against an attack by his political
antagonist Aeschines, illustrate the wide range of his
eloquence even on a single occasion. He attacks his rival's
speech:

> If my calumniator had been Aeacus, or Rhadamanthus,
> or Minos, instead of a mere scandal-monger, a market-
> place loafer, a poor devil of a clerk, he could hardly
> have used such language, or equipped himself with
> such offensive expressions. Hark to his melodramatic
> bombast: 'Oh, Earth! Oh, Sun! Oh, Virtue!', and all
> that vapouring; his appeals to 'intelligence and educa-
> tion, whereby we discriminate between things of good
> and evil report' – for that was the sort of rubbish you

111 Music and poetry played a leading part in education, though rhetoric was later added. In this early fifth-century school scene one boy is being taught to play the lyre, while another recites verses from the *Iliad*

112 In this Roman mosaic of the Academy at Athens Plato sits holding a stick, perhaps to draw a geometrical figure in the sand. A box on the ground contains a celestial sphere and a sundial stands behind. Note the Acropolis, top right

heard him spouting. Virtue! you runagate; what have you or your family to do with virtue? How do you distinguish between good and evil report? Where and how did you qualify as a moralist? Where did you get your right to talk about education?

Later he assures the jury that the policy of resistance to Macedon was in line with Athenian tradition:

Ill. 110

You cannot, men of Athens, you cannot have done wrongly when you accepted the risks of war for the redemption and the liberties of mankind; I swear it by our forefathers who bore the brunt of warfare at Marathon, who stood in array of battle at Plataea, who fought in the sea-fights of Salamis and Artemisium, and by all the brave men who repose in our public sepulchres, buried there by a country that accounted them all to be alike worthy of the same honour – all, I say, Aeschines, not the successful and the victorious alone. So justice bids: for by all the duty of brave men was accomplished: their fortune was such as Heaven severally allotted to them.

Ill. 111

Rhetoric was not confined to the law-courts and the Assembly but quickly spread to other fields, including some which traditionally belonged to poetry. Orations on philosophical or political topics became an alternative to drinking-songs at banquets. Festivals were now occasions not only for the recitations of rhapsodes, but for exhibition speeches in the grand manner. Instruction in the technique of speaking found a place alongside memorization of Homer in the schools. Such intensive cultivation of eloquence had an inevitable effect on prose style, reshaping it into an instrument of telling argument and appeal to the emotions. Numerous teachers of the new art in the fourth century built on the foundations laid by the Sophists in the fifth: the most important of

114–116 The portrait of Plato, *right*, inscribed with his name, is the most authentic we possess. The chief speaker in most of his dialogues is Socrates, who wrote nothing himself but provided the main inspiration for the extensive philosophical literature of the fourth and later centuries. The fresco below, bearing the name 'Socrates', was discovered in 1963 in a Roman house at Ephesus in Asia Minor. The statuette – a Roman copy of a fourth-century BC original – gives Socrates the picturesque ugliness, like that of the god Silenus, which is ascribed to him by Alcibiades in his vivid description of him in Plato's *Symposium*

117 A growing feature of Greek literature in the fourth century BC and later is the realistic representation of ordinary people and ordinary life, exemplified above all in comedy and the 'mime', with which both Plato's dialogues and the poems of Theocritus were connected. The same tendency is found in art. The lively comic statuette, *left*, is of a slave sitting on an altar, no doubt to escape a beating

them for the future of literature was Isocrates (436–338), no great orator himself (his numerous 'speeches' are tracts or essays written for readers rather than an audience) but the chief creator of rhetoric as a distinct science and chief architect of the 'grand style' which became the model for later Greek and Latin prose. He and his pupils were largely responsible for the extension of the influence of rhetoric not only to history and biography, but to nearly all branches of literature. From this time onwards eloquence, not truth or clarity, was the standard by which a writer was most commonly judged.

The Philosophers

In contrast with this trend stand two great collections of philosophical prose: the entire works of Plato (427–347), and a large part of the writings of Aristotle. A number of

Ill. 113

118

118 Terracotta figures of a well-dressed lady of the Hellenistic period and a maid-servant similar to those described by Theocritus. The figure of the maid-servant was found in Alexandria

earlier thinkers who wrote in prose or verse have already been mentioned, but nothing from any of them now exists in more than fragmentary form; and the same fate has overtaken most of the voluminous output of the founders of the later philosophical schools and their followers, until we come to Plotinus in the third century AD. Plato and Aristotle are the sole survivors from a branch of literature to which scores of authors contributed in ancient times.

Ill. 114

Plato, if we are to believe autobiographical information in a letter attributed to him, might himself have become a leading figure in the politics of his native Athens; but he turned away in disgust from the political atmosphere of the closing years of the Peloponnesian War, and the

Ills 115, 116

execution of Socrates in 399 BC and subsequent experiences in the West completed his aversion. One of the main aspects of contemporary life that he rejected was rhetoric, which he rightly regarded as an art concerned with show, not with reality. On more than one occasion he exposes the shallowness of contemporary eloquence by portraying Socrates as the true orator; in the *Apology*, for example, where Socrates also defends his own past before a mass jury, he replies to his accusers' allegation that he is a clever speaker:

> I have not the slightest skill as a speaker – unless, of course, by a skilful speaker they mean one who speaks the truth. If that is what they mean, I would agree that I am an orator, though not after their pattern.

Plato's main answer to the rhetoricians, however, was the dialogue form of his own works, to which he himself brought superb artistry of a different kind. Oratory had grown out of one side of the activities of the city-state – the importance of ability to sway an audience; in the dialogue Plato crystallized another aspect of Athenian daily life – conversation between individuals in the streets or the market-place, in which lay the possibility, as Socrates had shown, of the clash of mind on mind in a joint search for truth.

The dialogue was not the creation of Plato's genius alone. Prose 'mimes', as they were called – simple sketches of everyday talk – had been written in Sicily in the fifth century by Sophron and were said to have gained Plato's admiration. The habit of theoretical disputation was evidently common at Athens in the last decades of the century, and the Sophists and others may well have written representations of it: certainly it is repeatedly echoed in Thucydides and Euripides and Aristophanes. But it was the influence of Socrates, who himself wrote nothing, that brought the dialogue fully into being as a branch of literature. After his execution a number of his admirers – we hear of twelve, and there may have been more – sought to defend his memory by writing conversations in which he was the main speaker, although apart from those ascribed to Plato only three by Xenophon and fragments of others are now extant. A question incapable of solution is the relation of this type of literature to historical reality – the extent to which its portraits of Socrates and his contemporaries can be accepted as historically correct. Like the historical novel, the dialogue is probably better regarded as fiction, though it must often have had a considerable foundation in fact.

The chronology of Plato's dialogues is another puzzle, but stylistic tests point to certain groupings with which most scholars agree. His early writings are simple, brief, inconclusive: Socrates talks to Lysis about friendship, or demonstrates the mental confusions of Euthyphro on the subject of piety. Plato's achievement was the elaboration of this simple form into works which have greater literary appeal, as well as more philosophic value, than all the speeches of the orators. In the longer dialogues of his middle years the conversation is narrated instead of being set down like a play: the occasion and the characters are described, and we are presented with a series of portraits, admiring or satiric, which were the most brilliant product of the new biographical trend in literature. In addition Plato brings other elements within the dialogue framework: speeches which often contain subtle parody difficult for us to judge; stories or 'myths' introduced where reasoned discussion of a subject comes to an end and imagination, rising sometimes to great poetic heights, is the guide. The result is an amazing variety of content and style. The *Protagoras*, for example, is gentle comedy – a delightfully satirical picture of a gathering of the major Sophists in a wealthy house at Athens where they are visited by Socrates. The *Symposium* describes a drinking-party at which some of the most brilliant men of the day, including Aristophanes, compete in speeches on the subject of love, until Socrates (since he is himself no orator) recounts a speech he once heard which proves to be the most eloquent of them all; at the end the drunken Alcibiades breaks in and delivers a eulogy of Socrates, the embodiment of the highest love and of the superiority of wisdom over the flesh. Very different in mood, though probably written about the same time, is the *Phaedo* with its account of Socrates' last hours before his execution, spent in trying to convince his friends that his real self will survive: his own calmness in the face of death and the superbly simple narrative of his end dramatize the theme and lift it beyond the level of rational argument. Greatest of all the works of Plato's prime is the *Republic*, which describes Plato's ideal state but is by no means confined to politics. Socrates himself is the narrator of a conversation which becomes a search for the nature of justice in the individual and the state alike, and a revelation of the knowledge on which the wisdom of the philosopher-ruler and the happiness of all must depend.

It is the dialogues of this period that establish Plato as the greatest writer of Greek prose. In his later years he turned away from the richness and elaboration of such masterpieces and went back to the simple form, though not the brevity, of his early works. His concern now was with the philosophical problems that arose within his own school, the Academy; and usually Socrates is re- *Ill. 112* placed as chief speaker by a figure obviously representing Plato himself. The device of question and answer often wears very thin; and although the *Laws*, his last and longest work, is nominally a conversation, and the *Timaeus* consists mainly of a 'myth' of the creation of the world, both are in fact little different from lectures. These products of Plato's old age are full of significance for the development of his thought, but as literature they lack life because they are remote from the living environment in which the dialogue form arose.

Plato's students in the Academy followed his example by writing dialogues; among them, Aristotle, his greatest pupil. Unfortunately, Aristotle's early writings are now lost: if we may judge by the extant fragments of them and the verdict of ancient critics, they would have given him a high place in the history of Greek literature. The numerous treatises of his which do survive appear to be some sort of record of the lectures he gave in his philo-sophical school at Athens, the Lyceum; and although the brief and incomplete *Poetics* has had a profound influence on the literary ideas of the modern world, the rest belong to philosophy and science rather than to literature. Of the Greek philosophers time has preserved only Plato as a great figure in the history of literature as well as thought.

CHAPTER FIVE

After Alexander

The Impact of Macedon

Most of the literature so far described was the product of a single social pattern – the sovereign city-state, of which Athens was the outstanding example. But the fourth century was overshadowed by historical forces which spelt the doom of the independent city: Plato's rejection of contemporary politics and Demosthenes' appeals for a firm stand against the menace from the north are both signs of a growing crisis which culminated in the triumph of Macedon and the conquests of Alexander. Although the Athenians regarded the Macedonians as semi-barbarians, the result of their supremacy was not the end of Greek culture, but its spread. Throughout the Greek-speaking world, now greatly extended, conditions developed which the modern mind regards as favourable for the advance of literature: book production and the reading public increased; under wealthy patronage great *Ill. 119* libraries were established, festivals became more numerous and more lavish and fine buildings were erected to house them. From the large literary output of this Hellenistic Age – mostly prose, but also many types of verse – little now survives, although papyrus discoveries have added much during the past hundred years and more is being continually published.

119 Greek literature of the greatest period made its impact through the spoken word rather than through books, but in Hellenistic and Roman times book production was on a large scale and libraries a commonplace. Here a doctor sits reading a papyrus roll, the normal ancient book

The output of literature grew; but the genius which had thrown up one new form after another and produced such masterpieces within each had drawn its inspiration from the atmosphere of the city, and the great creative period ended with the decline of the sovereign power of the city-state. Political and social change brought no radically different literary forms into being, but only modifications of the old: the new outlook on life found its chief reflection, in literature as in art, in a new concern with personal life and emotion, a new realism in the portrayal of character. The writer now sees man as an individual rather than a citizen. The little book of *Characters* by the philosopher Theophrastus sets the tone for the new age, and romantic love becomes an accepted theme.

Athens remained the home of drama, although theatres and dramatic festivals were set up throughout the eastern Mediterranean. The contests in tragedy and comedy in the Theatre of Dionysus continued, but until the last decades of the fourth century we have only brief fragments of some of the plays presented. Comedy seems to have shown the greater vitality and power of development; and when Attic drama partially emerges again from

125

120–122 Our knowledge of the work of Menander was greatly increased by the recent discovery of a whole comedy, the *Dyskolos*, the last page of which is shown here, *left*. The author's name and the title of the play are written at the foot. The reliefs, *opposite*, represent Menander himself with comic masks and one of the Muses, and a scene from late comedy: a friend restrains a father's indignation as his son returns noisily from a feast

Ill. 120

Ill. 117

Ills 121, 122

obscurity, it is comedy that we can study. Papyrus finds have given us parts of several plays by Menander (342–291), acclaimed in antiquity as the outstanding playwright of his day, and in 1956 a whole play of his, the *Dyskolos* or the *Bad-Tempered Man*, came to light. These remains, like the works of Roman playwrights based on Menander, present us with a type of drama very different from Aristophanes, and perhaps more indebted to Euripides than to early comedy. The chorus has been reduced to a mere song-and-dance interlude, indicated by a stage-direction in the text. The language is neither fantastic nor obscene, but (although still in iambic verse) close to ordinary educated speech. There is no caricature of individuals; the characters are realistic portraits of types familiar in contemporary Athens: old men, erring sons, their womenfolk, and their dependants – servants, cooks, nurses, prostitutes, and the rest. A clever slave is often the most dynamic and amusing figure in the play. The plot is no longer farcical or extravagant, but a tale from normal life with love as its central theme and a happy ending assured. Menander's masked all-male actors in the open-air theatre would hardly have seemed realistic to a modern audience, but his realism astonished the Greeks; and through their Roman imitators he and his contemporaries gave to Europe the conception of the realistic comedy of manners.

The Scholar-Poets of Alexandria

Apart from drama and philosophy, Alexandria was the literary capital of the Hellenistic world. Alexander's new foundation in Egypt grew rapidly into a great multiracial community very different from Athens or the other old towns of Greece proper. Commerce, administration, and the professions were dominated by an upper class which was Greek in language and outlook, if not always by birth; and in control of all were the Macedonian Ptolemies and their court. This was not a society in whose life literature could play a central part: rather it depended for its existence on the patronage of the Ptolemies, who were anxious to add lustre to the brilliance of their régime and to prove that Macedonian 'barbarians' were as civilized as anyone of true Hellenic stock. To this end they established a magnificent 'Museum' or 'Hall of the Muses' in the royal quarter, and a great Library nearby to which their agents brought many thousands of papyrus rolls – a collection which, if it had survived, would have transformed our picture of Greek literature. Here was a tempting refuge for scholars and scientists from the disorders and disturbances of the time, and the Ptolemies' invitation attracted them to Alexandria from all parts of the Greek world except Athens. Some of them classified and edited the literature in the Library and so made more possible its preservation into modern times.

Men of such learning naturally wrote many books in prose – not oratory or philosophy, but technical and specialized disquisitions and handbooks such as the *Elements* of Euclid or Eratosthenes' *On the Measurement of the Earth*. But what we now possess is a slowly growing portion of the verse produced at Alexandria, remnants of a brief flowering of poetry between 290 and 240 BC. Its authors were scholar-poets, highly conscious of their art and much concerned with theories of how it should be exercised. Far from the mass audience at the Panathenaea or the Great Dionysia, they wrote for a select circle of listeners or readers; and for verse forms to suit such a purpose they turned chiefly to much earlier models – the short epic, the narrative elegy, the hymn, the epigram. They found traditional but novel subject-matter in unfamiliar legend drawn from local chronicles or little-known sections of the 'Epic Cycle'. Yet in their poetry also we find not only ingenuity and prettiness and wit, but realism, the expression of personal emotion, and other characteristic features of the time.

The most representative of the Alexandrian poets is Callimachus, a figure whose stature grows as nearly every year adds something to our remains of his verses. The six *Hymns* which survive complete combine mythology and flattery of Ptolemy in an amalgam which has little attraction for the modern reader, but as parts of his finer work have come to light they have revealed an unexpected range of content and versatility of style. Perhaps some of his epigrams have the most direct appeal today; certainly they exemplify that small-scale perfection which Callimachus made his literary ideal and championed against his critics in the Prologue to his own longest work, the *Aetia* or *Beginnings*:

> Go learn, O green-eyed monster's fatal brood,
> By Art, not parasangs, to judge what's good.
> Look not to me for lofty sounding song;

The thunder-claps to father Zeus belong.
When first a tablet on my knees reclined,
Apollo, lord of Lycia, spoke his mind:
'Give me, good bard, for sacrificial fare
A victim fat: but let your Muse be spare.
And listen – when your chariot skims the road,
Avoid the route that takes a wagon's load;
Leave open ways and trodden tracks alone,
And go the gate that's narrow, but your own.'
I tuned my quill, nor let the warning pass –
A sweet cicala, not a raucous ass.
Long ears and all, another bard shall bray;
Let me go light, and flit my dainty way.

The main target of Callimachus' strictures was Apollonius, called 'the Rhodian' because he withdrew from
Alexandria to live at Rhodes. Apollonius had the temerity
to write a narrative poem half the length of the *Odyssey*
on the adventures of the Argonauts – the first literary
epic still extant. The *Argonautica* is closely modelled on
Homer – metre, language, similes and all – but the story
is often clogged by too much learning and most of the
characters, divine and human, are colourless. The reader
is rescued from tedium in the third of the poem's four
books by a typically Hellenistic feature, nearer in spirit,
though not in form, to the modern novel than to Homer
or Hesiod – the romantic yet vivid picture of the young
Medea falling in love with Jason, which clearly influenced
Virgil in his portrait of Dido and Aeneas. Callimachus
won this bout, but the long epic survived to reappear
at Rome, and Apollonius showed that he too could write
an epigram:

Ill. 123

'Cesspool' and 'cheat' begin with C,
And so does 'crass stupidity'.
Who wrote *Beginnings* is the man
From whom the whole affair began.

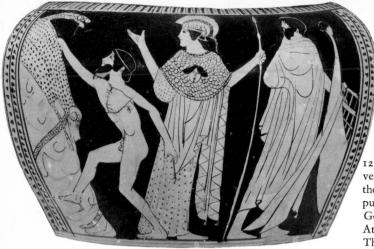

123 In this fifth-century version of the story of the Argonauts a rather puny Jason seizes the Golden Fleece watched by Athena and a comrade. The *Argo* is on the right

The Creator of the Pastoral

The greatest of the Alexandrians is Theocritus, creator of the pastoral – the one new poetic form, if such it can be called, in Hellenistic literature. In the hexameter pieces which later became known as his *Idylls* (the Greek word means 'short poems') the familiar Alexandrian features are again present, but they rarely spoil his poetry: he is erudite, but seldom displays his learning; he flatters his patrons and inserts open or veiled allusions to his friends and fellow-poets, but usually without striking a jarring note; his constant theme is romantic love, but he tempers it with realism and humour. The collection includes a variety of forms, skilfully adapted or sometimes combined together. Some of the poems are brief narratives in epic style. Others are sophisticated versions of the 'mime', which now became a vehicle of Hellenistic realism. Even Menander does not go so far in realistic portraiture as Theocritus' Syracusan women walking with their maids through the streets of Alexandria to visit the royal palace for the festival of Adonis:

Ill. 118

GORGO Praxinoa,
O, look at all that crowd before the door.
PRAXINOA Incredible. Here, Gorgo, take my arm,

and you catch hold of Eutychis there, Eunoa,
or you'll be separated – now let's try
to push in altogether. Mind, Eunoa,
keep hold of me – O, Gorgo, what a shame,
my summer cloak is torn from top to bottom.

This is a 'mime' of city life. Realism combined with
romance, and with country folk-song traditions that may
have included the singing-match and the refrain, to produce the pastorals, which have given us not only the
idealized peasant, not only Daphnis and Lycidas and
Amaryllis, but descriptions of nature hardly equalled in
Greek poetry.

In Roman Times

The *Idylls* were the last great achievement of Greek
poetry prior to the conquest of Greece by Rome. Thereafter most of what is best in classical literature comes from
Latin authors, following after their own fashion the lines
of development laid down by the Greeks. But the continued abundance and variety of Greek writing even in
the Roman period may be illustrated by mentioning a
few of the authors whose works, in whole or in part, have
survived: the historian Polybius, who under Roman
patronage took Thucydides as his chief model in describing the rise of Rome to imperial power; Plutarch, whose
Parallel Lives of Greek and Roman soldiers and statesmen
are the most famous product of that biographical writing
which had begun in the fourth century BC; Lucian,
master of the satiric dialogue, whose lively castigations
of cant and hypocrisy owed something to Aristophanes
as well as to Plato; Longus, author of the romance
Daphnis and Chloe, with its pastoral setting reminiscent
of Theocritus: even the modern novel has a prototype
among the Greeks. All these are prose writers; for although (as the *Palatine Anthology* of epigrams compiled

in the tenth century A D bears witness) the art of verse was still practised, and sometimes to admirable effect, prose was the prevailing form of Greek literature in this later period just as poetry had dominated its earlier and more brilliant centuries.

This book has been concerned with the literary achievements of the Greeks while they were still free from control by any non-Greek Power – for at this distance in time we can hardly accept the prejudice which placed Alexander or his Macedonian successors among the 'barbarians'. The coming of Roman supremacy in the second century B.C, the first of many periods of foreign domination of Greece, seems a fitting point at which to break off an account which could otherwise be continued indefinitely. If by Greek literature we mean literature in Greek, its history has no ending: it is still being written today. Yet in a sense the words may be said to have a still wider meaning. It may well be said that most of the literature of the modern world has been Greek, in that it has drawn its forms and inspiration, directly or indirectly, from the Greeks. Homer and Euripides and Plato live on not only through the preservation of their own works, but because their influence has shaped our whole literary heritage; and that is a legacy which will last as long as the civilization which it has helped to create.

Sources of Quotations

Where no translator's name is given, the translation is the author's own. *O.B.G.V.* refers to the *Oxford Book of Greek Verse in Translation*, published by the Clarendon Press.

page 11 Homer, *Iliad* I, 1–5
tr. F. L. Lucas (Dent)

23 Homer, *Iliad* VIII, 555–61
tr. Tennyson

29 Homer, *Odyssey* VIII, 65–73
tr. R. Fitzgerald (Heinemann)

40 Homer, *Iliad* XXII, 153–7
tr. W. Marris (O.U.P.)

42 Hesiod, *Works and Days*, 27–9

44 Archilochus, fr. 6
tr. W. Marris (*O.B.G.V.*)

46 Archilochus, fr. 60
tr. D. L. Page (*The Listener*, 1959)

46 Mimnermus, fr. 2
tr. J. A. Pott (*O.B.G.V.*)

46, 47 Theognis, 1197–200
tr. W. Marris (*O.B.G.V.*)

47 Xenophanes, frs. 11, 16, 15

48 Homer, *Iliad* XVIII, 569–72
tr. W. Marris (O.U.P.)

49 Alcman, fr. 1
tr. G. A. Highet (*O.B.G.V.*)

50 Alcaeus, fr. 160
tr. Easby-Smith

50 Alcaeus, fr. 335
tr. C. M. Bowra (*O.B.G.V.*)

53 Sappho, fr. 130
tr. C. M. Bowra (*O.B.G.V.*)

53 Sappho, fr. 150
tr. D. G. Rossetti

53 Anacreon, fr. 5
tr. T. F. Higham (*O.B.G.V.*)

56 Simonides, fr. 119
tr. Bowles

page 58 Pindar, *Pythian* I, 1–10
tr. H. T. Wade-Gery and C. M. Bowra (*O.B.G.V.*)

62 Plato, *Ion*, 535e

78 Herodotus VI, 21
tr. G. Rawlinson (Murray)

83 Aeschylus, *Libation-Bearers*, 896–906
tr. P. Vellacott (Penguin)

86 Sophocles, *Electra*, 1473–8
tr. E. F. Watling (Penguin)

88 Euripides, *Electra*, 1205–23
tr. P. Vellacott (Penguin)

91 Cratinus, fr. 71
tr. T. F. Higham (*O.B.C.V.*)

94 Aristophanes, *Birds*, 785–9
tr. B. B. Rogers (Bell)

96, 97 Aristophanes, *Frogs*, 171–7, 209–13, 1008–12
tr. D. Barrett (Penguin)

102 Hecataeus, fr. 332

108 Herodotus VIII, 8

109, 110 Thucydides, I, 22
tr. R. Warner (Penguin)

112 Gorgias, fr. 6

114, 116 Demosthenes, *On the Crown*, 127–8, 208
tr. J. H. Vince (Heinemann)

120 Plato, *Apology*, 17b
tr. H. Tredennick (Penguin)

128, 129 Callimachus, Prologue to *Aetia*,
tr. T. F. Higham (*O.B.G.V.*)

129 *Palatine Anthology* XI, 275
tr. C. F. Angus

130, 131 Theocritus XV, 65–70
tr. J. Lindsay (*O.B.G.V.*)

Chronology

Many of the dates given are necessarily conjectural or approximate. Most authors' dates mark their *floruit*—about their fortieth year.

EVENTS		LITERATURE	
BC		**BC**	
3000	Bronze Age begins in Greece		
2000	Greek-speaking peoples enter Greece		
1700	Minoan sea-empire at its height		
1500	Rise of Mycenae	1500–1200	Linear B tablets
1300	Hittite texts refer to Achaeans		
1200	Fall of Troy		
1100	Dorian invasion		
		900–800	Introduction of alphabet
776	First Olympic Games	800–700	*Iliad* and *Odyssey*
750–500	Colonization		Hesiod
		648	Archilochus
630	Sparta crushes Messenian revolt		Alcman
594	Solon's reforms at Athens	580	Alcaeus and Sappho
560–527	Pisistratus 'tyrant' at Athens	544	Theognis
			Beginnings of Attic tragedy
		530	Anacreon
507	Cleisthenes' democratic reforms at Athens	515	Simonides
490–479	Persian Wars	490	Hecataeus
		486	Contests in comedy begin at Athens
		485	Aeschylus
			Birth of Protagoras, the first Sophist
479–454	Creation of Athenian Empire	478	Pindar
461	Pericles in power	456	Sophocles
447–432	Building of Parthenon	445	Herodotus
			Euripides
431–404	Peloponnesian War	429	Hippocrates
		427	Gorgias speaks at Athens
		420	Thucydides
		410	Aristophanes
399	Execution of Socrates	396	Isocrates
		390	Xenophon
		387	Plato
359–336	Philip king of Macedon		
		344	Aristotle
			Demosthenes
338	Philip victorious at Chaeronea		
336–323	Alexander king of Macedon		
331	Foundation of Alexnadria		
		302	Menander

EVENTS	LITERATURE
B C	B C
	270 Theocritus
	265 Callimachus
	255 Apollonius
200 Roman conquest of Greece begins	
	163 Polybius
31 Augustus master of the Graeco- Roman world	
	A D 86 Plutarch
	A D 160 Lucian

The Extant Plays

Aeschylus (525-456)

Persians	472	Agamemnon	458
Seven against Thebes	467	Libation-Bearers	458
Suppliant Women	463	Eumenides	458
Prometheus Bound			

Sophocles (496-406)

Ajax		Electra	
Antigone	441	Philoctetes	409
Women of Trachis		Oedipus at Colonus	
Oedipus the King			

Euripides (485-406)

Alcestis	438	Electra	413
Medea	431	Helen	412
Hippolytus	428	Ion	
Children of Heracles		Iphigenia among the Taurians	
Hecuba		Phoenician Women	
Suppliant Women		Orestes	408
Andromache		Bacchae	406
Mad Heracles	415	Iphigenia at Aulis	406
Trojan Women			

Satyr-play: Cyclops
Attributed to Euripides: Rhesus

Aristophanes (450-385)

Acharnians	425	Lysistrata	411
Knights	424	Women Celebrating the Thesmophoria	411
Clouds	423	Frogs	405
Wasps	422	Women in Parliament	391
Peace	421	Plutus	388
Birds	414		

Menander (342-291)

The Bad-Tempered Man	316

Bibliography

Translations

Recent years have seen the production of translations of Greek literature far too numerous for individual mention. The most complete series is the Loeb Classical Library (Heinemann, London), with Greek and English on opposite pages. There are many translations from the Greek in Everyman's Library (Dent, London) and the Penguin Classics. A valuable anthology is the *Oxford Book of Greek Verse in Translation*.

Notable recent translations of particular authors include versions of Aristophanes by D. Fitts, Homer's *Odyssey* by R. Fitzgerald (London, 1962), *The Complete Greek Tragedies* in nine volumes edited by D. Grene and R. Lattimore (Chicago, 1953–59), and R. Lattimore's *Odes of Pindar* (Chicago, 1947) and *Iliad* (Chicago, 1951).

General

BALDRY, H. C.   *Greek Literature for the Modern Reader*, Cambridge, 1951.
BOWRA, C. M.   *Ancient Greek Literature*, London, 1933.
——   *Landmarks in Greek Literature*, London, 1966.
LESKY, A.   *A History of Greek Literature*, English tr., London, 1966.
ROSE, H. J.   *A Handbook of Greek Literature*, 4th ed., London, 1950.
SCHEFOLD, K.   *Myth and Legend in Early Greek Art*, London, 1966.
WEBSTER, T. B. L.   *Greek Art and Literature*, 530–400 BC, Oxford, 1939.
——   *Art and Literature in Fourth Century Athens*, London, 1956.

Epic Poetry

BLEGEN, C. W.   *Troy and the Trojans*, London, 1963.
BOWRA, C. M.   *Tradition and Design in the Iliad*, London, 1930.
FINLEY, M. I.   *The World of Odysseus*, London, 1956.
KIRK, G. S.   *The Songs of Homer*, Cambridge, 1962.
LORIMER, H. L.   *Homer and the Monuments*, London, 1950.
NILSSON, M. P.   *Homer and Mycenae*, London, 1933.
PAGE, D. L.   *History and the Homeric Iliad*, California, 1959.

Lyric Poetry

BOWRA, C. M.   *Early Greek Elegists*, reprint, London, 1959.
——   *Greek Lyric Poetry*, 2nd ed., London, 1961.
——   *Pindar*, London, 1964.
BURN, A. R.   *The Lyric Age of Greece*, London, 1960.
PAGE, D. L.   *Sappho and Alcaeus*, Oxford, 1955.

Drama

ARNOTT, P. D.   *An Introduction to the Greek Theatre*, London, 1962.
BIEBER, M.   *The History of the Greek and Roman Theater*, 2nd ed., Princeton, 1961.
GRUBE, G. M. A.   *The Drama of Euripides*, London, 1941.
KITTO, H. D. F.   *Greek Tragedy*, 2nd ed., London, 1950.
LATTIMORE, R.   *The Poetry of Greek Tragedy*, Baltimore, 1958.
LESKY, A.   *Greek Tragedy*, English tr., London, 1965.

LUCAS, D. W.   *The Greek Tragic Poets*, London, 1950.
MURRAY, G.   *Aeschylus the Creator of Tragedy*, Oxford, 1940.
——— *Aristophanes*, Oxford, 1933.
——— *Euripides and his Age*, 2nd ed., Oxford, 1946.
PICKARD-CAMBRIDGE, A. W.   *Dithyramb, Tragedy and Comedy*, 2nd ed., Oxford, 1962.
——— *The Dramatic Festivals of Athens*, Oxford, 1953.
——— *The Theatre of Dionysus in Athens*, Oxford, 1946.
THOMSON, G.   *Aeschylus and Athens*, 2nd ed., London, 1948.
WALDOCK, A. J. A.   *Sophocles the Dramatist*, Cambridge, 1951.
WEBSTER, T. B. L.   *Greek Theatre Production*, London, 1956.
WHITMAN, C. H.   *Aristophanes and the Comic Hero*, Cambridge, Mass., 1964.

Prose

ADCOCK, F. E.   *Thucydides and his History*, Cambridge, 1963.
BURY, J. B.   *The Ancient Greek Historians*, reprint, New York, 1958.
DOBSON, J. F.   *The Greek Orators*, London, 1919.
FARRINGTON, B.   *Aristotle*, London, 1965.
FIELD, G. C.   *Plato and his Contemporaries*, London, 1930.
FINLEY, J. H.   *Thucydides*, Cambridge, Mass., 1942.
GLOVER, T. R.   *Herodotus*, California, 1924.
MYRES, J. L.   *Herodotus, Father of History*, Oxford, 1953.
PICKARD-CAMBRIDGE, A. W.   *Demosthenes and the Last Days of Greek Freedom*, New York, 1914.
TAYLOR, A. E.   *Plato, the Man and his Work*, London, 1926.

After Alexander

COUAT, A.   *Alexandrian Poetry*, London, 1931.
KÖRTE, A.   *Hellenistic Poetry*, Columbia, 1929.
WEBSTER, T. B. L.   *Hellenistic Poetry and Art*, London, 1964.
WRIGHT, F. A.   *A History of Later Greek Literature*, London, 1932.

List of Illustrations

The author and publishers are grateful to the many official bodies, institutions and individuals mentioned below for their assistance in supplying illustration material. Illustrations without acknowledgement are from originals in the archives of Thames and Hudson.

27 Seated Muse. Athenian white-ground lekythos from Attica. Lugano, von Schoen collection

28 Ambushing of Dolon. Red-figure krater. British Museum. Photo courtesy of the Trustees of the British Museum

29 Tablet with Hittite inscription from Ḫattušaš (Boghazköy)

30 Map showing the Greek and Trojan allies

31 Ivory plaque with warrior from Delos. Delos Museum. Photo courtesy French School of Archaeology, Athens

32 Reconstructed boars' tusk helmet from a tomb near Knossos. Herakleion Museum. Photo Peter Clayton

33 House in Troy VIIA. Photo courtesy of Department of Classics, University of Cincinnati

34 Walls of Troy, detail from François Vase. Museo Archeologico, Florence

35 Silver 'siege' rhyton from Mycenae. National Museum, Athens

36 Trojan Horse, detail of relief amphora from Mykonos. Mykonos Museum. Photo German Archaeological Institute, Athens

37 Hector and Andromache's farewell. Chalcidian krater from Vulci. Martin von Wagner Museum, Wurzburg

38 Death of Achilles. Black-figure amphora (now lost)

39 Hermes and cows of Apollo. Caeretan hydria. Louvre. Photo Giraudon

40 Farming scene. Black-figure vase. British Museum. Photo courtesy of the Trustees of the British Museum

41 Greek hoplite and Scythian mercenary. Attic black-figure amphora. Staatliche Museen, Berlin

42 Inscribed Attic Geometric jug. National Museum, Athens

43,44 Chorus of youths and maidens. Attic Geometric amphora. National Museum, Athens

45 Dancing girl and boy. Volute-krater from Ceglie del Campo. Museo Archeologico Nationale, Taranto. Photo Carrano Gennaro

46 Boys dancing to a flute. Boeotian jug from the Cabiri Sanctuary, Thebes. Staatliche Museen, Berlin

47 Sappho and Alcaeus. Red-figure vase. Antikensammlungen, Munich. Photo Uni Dia Verlag

48 Man ladling wine at a party. Black-figure oinochoe. National Museum, Athens

49 Girl picking an apple. Athenian cup. British Museum. Photo courtesy of the Trustees of the British Museum

50 Anacreon and companions. Attic lekythos. Museo Archeologico Nationale, Syracuse

51 Men in women's dress. Red-figure krater. Cleveland Museum of Art

52 Runners. Black-figure vase

53 Stadium, Delphi. Photo Rosemarie Pierer

54 Chariot race. Reverse of a silver tetradrachm of Syracuse. British Museum

55 Chariot racing. Vase lid. Museum Antiker Kleinkunst, Munich

56 Athenian Acropolis from the Pnyx. Photo Peter Clayton

57 Parthenon from north-west

58 Panathenaic Procession, west frieze of Parthenon

59 Dionysus feast with Lenae before idol. Red-figure hydria. Museo Archeologico Nationale, Naples

60 Reveller returning from the festival of the Anthesteria. Red-figure oinochoe. Metropolitan Museum of Art, Fletcher Fund, 1937

61 Sea-voyage of Dionysus illustrating Homeric Hymn. Antikensammlungen, Munich

62 Theatre of Dionysus, Athens. Photo Miss G. Farnell

63 Athenian bronze coin with Theatre of Dionysus and drawing of same. British Museum. Photo Peter Clayton

64 Stage front of Theatre of Dionysus, Athens. Photo Peter Clayton

65 High Priest's throne, Theatre of Dionysus, Athens. Photo Mansell

66 Greek bronze theatre tickets. After Bieber

67 Modern performance in Theatre of Epidaurus. Photo D. A. Harrissiadis

68 Stage scenery and figures. Krater fragment from Taranto. Martin von Wagner Museum, Würzburg. Photo E. Zwicker

69 Theatre of Epidaurus. Photo Peter Clayton

70 Costumed actor holding mask. Krater fragment from Taranto. Martin von Wagner Museum, Würzburg. Photo E. Zwicker

71 Terracotta figurine of an actor dressed as the heroine. British Museum. Photo Peter Clayton

72 Actors with masks. Detail of the Pronomos Vase. Museo Archeologico Nationale, Naples

73 Ivory statuette of tragic actor. Musée de Petit Palais, Paris. Photo Archive

74 Satyrs vintaging. Antikenmuseum, Basle

75 Funeral games of Patroclus. Fragment of a mixing-bowl. National Museum, Athens

76 Marble herm of Euripides. Mantua Museum

77 Bronze bust thought to be Sophocles. From Constantinople. British Museum. Photo courtesy of the Trustees of the British Museum

78 Suicide of Ajax. Bronze statuette from Populonia. Museo Archeologico, Florence

79 Murder of Agamemnon. Bronze shield-mount. Olympia Museum

80 Murder of Aegisthus. Bronze shield-mount. Olympia Museum

81,82 Murder of Agamemnon, and of Aegisthus. Both sides of a red-figure kalyx-krater. Photo courtesy Museum of Fine Arts, Boston. William Francis Warden Fund

83 Clytemnestra. Red-figure kylix. Staatliche Museen, Berlin

84 Clytemnestra killing Cassandra. Red-figure bowl. Museo Archeologico Nationale, Ferrara

85,86 Pylades restraining Clytemnestra, and Orestes killing Aegisthus. Red-figure pelike. Kunsthistorisches Museum, Vienna

87 Orestes at Delphi. Red-figure volute-krater. Museo Nationale, Naples

88 Terracotta figure of a grotesque actor. Staatliche Museen, Berlin

89 Terracotta group of actors. Martin von Wagner Museum, Würzburg

90 Hellenistic bronze tragic mask, from Piraeus. National Museum, Athens

91 Hellenistic terracotta comic mask, from Melos. British Museum. Photo courtesy of the Trustees of the British Museum

92 Men dressed as cocks. Red-figure amphora. Staatliche Museen, Berlin

93 Men dressed as horses. Red-figure amphora. Staatliche Museen, Berlin

94 Men dressed as birds. Black-figure oinochoe. British Museum. Photo courtesy of the Trustees of the British Museum

95 Fresco of a procession of donkey-headed figures, from Mycenae. National Museum, Athens

96 Hercules and Cerberus. Caeretan black-figure hydria from Cervetori. Louvre

97 Aesop and fox. Red-figure kylix. Vatican Museum. Photo Mansell-Alinari

98 Tree of Hippocrates, Cos. Photo Peter Clayton

99 Herm of Herodotus. Capitoline Museum, Rome. Photo Mansell-Anderson

100 Darius and messenger. Red-figure amphora from Canosa. Museo Nazionale, Naples. Photo Mansell-Alinari

101 Croesus on funeral pyre. Red-figure amphora from Vulci. Louvre

102 Greek attacking a Persian. Red-figure neck amphora from Rhodes. Metropolitan Museum of Art, Rogers Fund, 1906

103 Scythian tomb, Kostromskaya, South Russia

104 Frozen burial, tomb 5 Pazyrk. Photo courtesy of Dr R. D. Barnett

105,106 Electrum vase from Kul Oba. State Hermitage, Leningrad. From an electrotype in the Victoria and Albert Museum. Photos Peter Clayton

107 Map of the world known to Herodotus

108 Marble herm of Pericles, from Tivoli. British Museum. Photo courtesy of the Trustees of the British Museum

109 Demosthenes. Vatican Museum. Photo German Archaeological Institute, Rome

110 Cerameikos, Athens. Photo Peter Clayton

111 School scene. Red-figure kylix from Cerveteri. Staatliche Museen, Berlin

112 Plato's Academy. Mosaic from a villa near Pompeii. Museo Nazionale, Naples. Photo Andre Held

113 Marble head of Aristotle. Kunsthistoriches Museum, Vienna

114 Marble herm of Plato. Staatliche Museen, Berlin

115 Wall-painting of Socrates, from Ephesus. Photo Haber Ajansi, Istanbul

116 Marble statue of Socrates. British Museum. Photo courtesy of the Trustees of the British Museum

117 Comic terracotta of a slave seated on an altar. British Museum. Photo Peter Clayton

118 Tanagra terracotta lady. British Museum. Photo Peter Clayton

119 Relief of a doctor. Ostia Museum

120 Ms of *Dyskolos* by Menander. Bibliotheque Bodmer, Geneva

121 Marble relief of Menander and New Comedy masks. Lateran Museum, Rome. Photo Mansell-Anderson

122 Marble relief of scene from New Comedy. Museo Nazionale, Naples. Photo Mansell-Alinari

123 Jason and the Golden Fleece. Red-figure column krater. Metropolitan Museum of Art, New York, Harris Brisbane Dick Fund, 1934

Index

Numbers in italics refer to illustrations